The Four Questions Every Monitoring Engineer is Asked

by Leon Adato,
with Rabbi Raphael Davidovich
Copyright 2019 Leon Adato

Copyrights, & Disclaimers

The Four Questions of Monitoring
By Leon Adato with Rabbi Raphael Davidovich
Copyright © 2019 All rights reserved

Editor: Ann Guidry
Special Content Review: Yechiel Kalmenson
Author photograph: Rene Lego
Cover Design: Copyright © 2019 by Masek Creative

Printing History:
April 2019 - First Edition

Table of Contents

Acknowledgements

Hashem, my own words fail me, and I am thankful that Chazal has provided me with a meager expression of thanks to put here, from the words we pray each Shabbat morning,

> *"Were our mouth as full of song as the sea, and our tongue as full of joyous song as its multitude of waves, and our lips as full of praise as the breadth of the heavens, and our eyes as brilliant as the sun and the moon, and our hands as outspread as eagles of the sky and our feet as swift as hinds - we still could not thank You sufficiently..."*

So many people helped make this book a reality, and I'm overwhelmed by the generosity, compassion, patience, and support I've been gifted. The task of ensuring that each person is thanked appropriately is, I fear, beyond my abilities. So, if you do not see your name here, please know that I thank you in my heart, despite being accidentally omitted from this page.

My family is such a constant source of strength and purpose and joy. They are the reason I'm able to face the day each morning, and they are what I thank Hashem for last when I lay down to sleep. Thank you for being patient with my absences (mental or geographic) as I worked to see this book come to fruition.

I consider myself lucky to count Ann Guidry, the editor of this work, as a colleague, advisor, mentor, and a friend. Her gentle and persistent hand is behind so many of the things I've written, and I would entrust this book to nobody else. Thank you for making the time to help keep my thoughts clear and concise (well, more concise than they would have been otherwise).

While Yechiel Kalmenson and I have never met face to face, I never the less feel a bond with him as he is both a co-religionist and a comrade-at-arms in the IT trenches. He is one of the few people I know who was able to take both the technical and religious ideas I've laid out and point out a mis-attributed a concept, where analogies fell short, or where I missed an opportunity to make things clearer.

Rob Masek and I have worked together on various projects for almost a decade, and I'm continuously impressed by his ability to take my nearly-unintelligible concepts and turn them into beautiful visual works of art. Thank you for creating a cover that is truly eye-catching.

Everyone at SolarWinds (especially my co-Head Geeks) are a constant source of ideas, excitement, and insight. Their appetite for new knowledge and their willingness to dive into all things tech is what pushes me to improve myself every single day.

Finally, to the many people who offered their time and wisdom to proofread, share their ideas, or just listen to me babble at them as I worked out the concepts that would eventually become the book you are holding in your hands.

But most of all, I wish a heartfelt "thank you" to all of you who are holding this book in their hands and sharing some of your time with me as you read this. Being an orthodox Jew working in IT, I find that people around me understand either one half of my life or the other, but rarely both. Which means I spend a lot of time either explaining "geek" culture (computers, code, and/or comic books) to my co-religionists; or breaking down Jewish culture (halakhot, chagim, and/or what time Shabbat starts this week) to my work colleagues. Writing this book gave me a chance to unite multiple aspects of my life, education, and personality into a single piece in a way that I don't often have the chance to do otherwise.

Dedications

To Debbie

In these pages are stories and ideas taken from the very earliest moments of our journey together. Just as those experiences have shaped us as a couple, so too have you shaped me as a person. While I am able to offer answers to The Four Questions of Monitoring, the question I find I cannot answer is, "What would life be like without you?" You were simply always there. You are, and always shall be, my best friend.

To Heather, Isabelle, Natan, and Raphael

As children, you pushed me, both by your words and your actions, to consider a life I could never have imagined otherwise. You effortlessly demonstrated a depth of faith and a willingness to learn that left me no choice but to follow in your wake. It quickly became clear who was the teacher and who the student. Now that you are grown, I am simultaneously proud of everything you have accomplished and humbled by your willingness to include me in your journeys.

Is This Book For You?

This guide was written to provide insight into the questions and challenges monitoring engineers face as they create and maintain a monitoring solution in a corporate environment. It is geared for IT professionals — people who create, maintain, and support computer systems and their users — who know what monitoring is capable of, and who may or may not have hands-on experience with monitoring software.

If you find yourself interested in this topic but feel a bit behind on the details, I've written a few other free guides that can help.

- Monitoring 101:
  https://www.solarwinds.com/resources/whitepaper/monitoring-101
- Monitoring 201:
  https://www.solarwinds.com/resources/ebook/monitoring-201
- Automation, Not Art:
  https://www.solarwinds.com/resources/ebook/its-automation-not-art

Meanwhile, this completely tool-agnostic guide will not ask you to actually dive into monitoring automation using software package XYZ. But it is my hope that after reading this, when you do start setting up automation using monitoring software XYZ, some of the functions will be less arcane.

Introduction

A Note to the Wary

In this book, I make liberal use of ideas, anecdotes, and examples from the Jewish tradition. Because religion can be a touchy subject for many of us, I'd like to offer a few assurances:

First, Judaism does not have a tradition of proselytizing. At no point will this book suggest that you should consider "joining the team."

Second, while I find religion in general (and Judaism specifically) adds a unique frame of reference for my work life, I recognize and respect that this isn't true for everyone. If you find the talk of Jewish traditions to be off-putting, I've made it easy for you to skip ahead to the next "regular" technical part of the book. Sections that involve faith-based ideas are marked like this:

> This is some Jewish content

You can simply pass over (see what I did there?) those sections and on to the technical bits.

This book is also about monitoring, a topic that some hold a nearly religious fervor about. It is not, however, about monitoring with any particular product. All the ideas, techniques, and concepts apply, regardless of which solution you have, wish you had, use, or love. Just as I'm not trying to foist my religious views on anyone, neither am I trying to push any vendor's agenda or make a thinly veiled sales pitch when you least expect it.

Every Conversation Begins With a Question

Once a year, Jews around the world gather together to celebrate Pesach (also known as "Passover," "The Feast of Matzah," or even "The Feast of the Paschal Lamb"). More a ceremonial meal than actual "feast," this gathering of family and friends can last until the wee hours of the morning. The dinnertime dialogue follows a prescribed order (or "seder," which actually means "order" in Hebrew) that runs the gamut from leader-led prayers to storytelling to group sing-alongs to question-and-answer sessions and even—in some households—a dramatized retelling of the exodus narrative replete with jumping rubber frogs, ping-pong ball hail stones, and wild animal masks.

At the heart of it all, the Seder is designed to do exactly one thing: to get the people at the table to ask questions. Questions like, "Why do we do that? What does this mean? Where did this tradition come from?" To emphasize: the Seder is not meant to answer questions, but rather provoke them.

Judaism is a religion that seems to love questions (and the explanations, debates, and discussions they lead to) more than the answers themselves. I'm fond of telling coworkers that the answer to any question about Judaism begins with the words, "Well, that depends..." and ends two hours later when you have three more questions than when you started.

The fact that I grew up in an environment with such fondness for questions may be what led me to pursue a career in IT, and to specialize in monitoring. More on that in a bit.

But the ability to ask questions is nothing by itself. An old proverb says, "One fool can ask more questions than seven wise men can answer." And that brings me back to the Pesach Seder. Near the start of the Seder meal, the youngest person at the table is invited to ask the Four Questions. They begin with question, "Why is this night different from all other nights?" The conversation proceeds to observe some of the ways that the Pesach meal has taken a normal mealtime practice and changed it so that it's off-kilter, abnormal, noticeably different. For example, "Why," asks one of the questions, "on most other nights do we not dip our food even once, but tonight we dip twice?"

Like many Jewish traditions, the reasoning behind the Four Questions has a simple answer, but that's not where it ends. If you dig just a bit you find additional reasons that go surprisingly deep. As I said, at the surface, it's done to demonstrate to children that questions are welcome. It's a way of inviting everyone at the table to take stock of what is happening and ask about anything unfamiliar.

But the deeper message speaks to the nature of questions, and the responsibility of those who are expected to answer. "Be prepared," it seems to say. "Questions can come from anywhere, about anything. Be willing to listen. Be willing to think before you speak. Be willing to say, 'I don't know, but let's find out!'" The Four Questions also teaches us to be willing to look past trite answers. To be ready to reconsider, and to defend our position with facts. And perhaps most wonderfully of all, to be prepared to switch, at a moment's notice, from someone who answers, to someone who asks.

Once again, I believe that being exposed to this tradition of open honesty and curiosity is what made (and still makes) the discipline of monitoring resonate for me.

It's also, obviously, what provided the inspiration for the title of this book.

Over the years, I've had the chance to set up monitoring solutions for a variety of companies, targeted at a range of situations. A pattern of questions emerged among project stakeholders, departmental colleagues, and the consumers of the data that my monitoring solution produced. I began to think of these questions as "The Four Questions (of monitoring)," and over time I've realized that a successful monitoring implementation is one which is ready to address those questions. I also noticed that the monitoring implementations that struggled, often did so because they were not prepared to answer those same questions.

So, you hold the key in your hands. In this book, I've laid out the Four Questions of Monitoring before you like a well-set table, along with my thoughts about why they are asked and what, as a monitoring specialist, you need to have in place to provide satisfying answers.

About Names

As I reference Jewish concepts in general and Pesach specifically, I've chosen to use the English transliteration of Hebrew words for people and places and things, offering the common English usage the first time (you can also find them compiled in an appendix at the end of this book). Thus, "Passover" becomes "Pesach", "Egypt" is referred to as "Mitzrayim", "Jacob" is rendered as "Yaakov", and so on.

While I recognize that many readers will not be familiar with these Hebrew terms, and that doing may even interrupt the flow of the text for some, I feel other, more important considerations are at stake:

First, these are the actual, original names of these people, places, and things. English speakers may know the first woman as "Eve", which is how the Greeks translated it, but it is "Chavah" in the original text of the Torah, and I have always felt that using someone's proper name is always more respectful.

Second, using the Hebrew words conveys an authenticity, an un-filtered-ness, to the anecdotes and plot points I'm sharing. I also hope it provides a window into a culture that may be different than that of the reader.

Finally, Hebrew words carry essential meanings that go beyond "that is the name of so-and-so." The names of key figures and places in Torah tell their own story. When we read that Rebecca gave birth to twins, first Esau and then Jacob, the Hebrew listener understands that Rivka ("to join") gave birth to Esav ("red", "hairy") and then Yaakov ("heel-grabber"). The essence of the character is embedded in the name of the person, place, or thing.

Here's a sample:

English Name	Hebrew Name	Hebrew Meaning
Eve	Chavah	Source of life
Isaac	Yitzchak	He will laugh (rejoice)
Rebecca	Rivka	"join" or "connect"
Jacob	Yaakov	Heel-grabber
Esau	Esav	"Red", or "hairy"
Joseph	Yosef	He will increase
Passover	Pesach	"Jumped over" or "Skipped"
Egypt	Mitzrayim	The narrow place

The last word, Mitzrayim (Egypt), is perhaps the most compelling reason for my choice to use the Hebrew versions. In the Pesach story, we read how B'nei Yisrael (the house-of-struggles-with-the-Divine, i.e.: the Israelites) were enslaved, trapped in Mitzrayim (the narrow place, i.e.: Egypt) and how they passed through the waters of the Yam Suf (Red Sea) to freedom.

Once we know the meaning of the words, we see an entity trapped in a narrow place, struggling to escape, passing through waters to freedom. The Exodus narrative is quite literally telling the story of the birth of a nation.

Are any of these points relevant to monitoring or the work of IT professionals? As I mentioned at the start of this chapter, "that depends." To explain why, I'll end with a personal story deeply embedded in the technical world:

Early in my career as a monitoring engineer, I was having problems with a particular piece of software. I was making "folders" (containers, really) to group my monitored objects. I wanted to be organized, so I created master folders, into which I would put sub-folders. In those I would also put sub-folders, and so on.

Inevitably, the system would crash catastrophically, and I would have to re-install everything from scratch. By my fourth re-install, I was feeling both angry and confused.

I reached out to my friend Doug, who didn't have experience with this particular program, but knew all sorts of odd things and was a great sounding board for me when I was stuck. Without missing a beat, he asked, "did you create more than 3 levels of containers?"

"Yes"

"Well of course it crashed. This software is based on CORBA. The CORBA database model can only handle 3 levels of containership before it corrupts."

I hadn't even realized the software was based on CORBA, let alone the limitations of the CORBA model.

It turns out that knowing the true name and the history of a thing can lead to powerful insights about how it operates and what its limitations may be.

About the Four Questions

מַה נִּשְׁתַּנָּה, הַלַּיְלָה הַזֶּה מִכָּל הַלֵּילוֹת

שֶׁבְּכָל הַלֵּילוֹת אָנוּ אוֹכְלִין חָמֵץ וּמַצָּה הַלַּיְלָה הַזֶּה, כֻּלּוֹ מַצָּה

שֶׁבְּכָל הַלֵּילוֹת אָנוּ אוֹכְלִין שְׁאָר יְרָקוֹת הַלַּיְלָה הַזֶּה, מָרוֹר

שֶׁבְּכָל הַלֵּילוֹת אֵין אָנוּ מַטְבִּילִין אֲפִילוּ פַּעַם אֶחָת הַלַּיְלָה הַזֶּה, שְׁתֵּי פְעָמִים

שֶׁבְּכָל הַלֵּילוֹת אָנוּ אוֹכְלִין בֵּין יוֹשְׁבִין וּבֵין מְסַבִּין הַלַּיְלָה הַזֶּה, כֻּלָּנוּ מְסַבִּין

Why is this night different from all the other nights?
That on all other nights we eat both chametz and matzah. On this night, we eat only matzah.
That on all other nights we eat many vegetables. On this night, maror.
That in all other nights we do not dip vegetables even once. On this night, we dip twice.
That in all other nights some eat sitting, and others reclining. On this night, we are all reclining.

Sharp-eyed readers will recognize that the four questions of the Pesach (Passover) Seder are actually one question with four observations and answers. But it's easy to see that these observations and answers are somewhat rhetorical. The implied follow-up question to each observation is, "Why? Why are we doing these things?"

Judaism encourages questions because it recognizes that the journey to a lifetime of answers must necessarily start with a question. If an individual isn't curious about a topic, the answers can be staring them in the face and it won't matter.

In Yeshivah—a day-school system for Jewish children that combines secular and religious learning—the highest praise one can receive is, "Du fregst a gutte kasha!" which is Yiddish for, "You ask a good question!"

Rabbi Abraham Twersky elaborates on this value in the following story. He says that when he was young, his teacher would relish challenges to his arguments. In his broken English, the teacher would say, "You right! You 100 prozent right! Now, I show you where you wrong."

This culture of questioning does not impact religious thinking alone. People who follow this system find that it extends to all areas of life.

Isidor Isaac Rabi won the Nobel Prize in Physics in 1944. When he was asked why he wanted to become a scientist, he answered, "My mother made me a scientist without ever intending it. Every other mother in Brooklyn would ask her child after school, 'So? Did you learn anything today?' But not my mother. She always asked me, 'Did you ask a good question today?' That difference—asking good questions—made me become a scientist!"

The lesson for us, as monitoring professionals, is twofold.

First, we need to foster that same sense of curiosity, that same willingness to ask questions, even when we think the answers may be a long time in coming. We need to question our own assumptions. We need to relish the experience of asking, so that it pushes us past the comfortable inertia of believing we already have an answer.

Second, we need to find ways to invite questions from our colleagues, as well. Like the Seder, we may have to present information in a way that is shocking, noticeable, and engaging, so that people are pushed beyond their own inherent shyness (or even apathy) to ask, "What is that all about?"

Most people who work in monitoring don't set out with that intent. Most of us are, by and large, network engineers, sysadmins, storage architects, or even infosec professionals. But in the course of our workday, we find ourselves wanting (or more likely needing) to know about the health of our environment. Therefore, we create or adopt tools to help us do that.

And then, surprise! We discover that the tools and techniques, not to mention the results, end up being interesting, engaging, and even fun. We extend our tools, develop our techniques, and see just how far the rabbit hole we created can go.

Later, someone else notices what we've built. Maybe it's because we start sending them the alerts we've been getting. Or they see a report that we used to explain a certain business-impacting event. Or they wonder how we can be so on top of things all the time. We seem to have all the answers at our fingertips.

When other people start to notice what we've done or discovered, there's a very good chance that they will ask us to do the same for them. They'll want our help to see inside the black box of their architecture; to help them detect an anomaly faster; to understand a recent system failure in greater detail. We become a monitoring engineer the moment we set our feet on that path.

This is the moment we make the leap from watching systems we care about, to monitoring systems that other people care about.

When we are doing it for our self, it's all about ease of maintenance, getting good (meaning useful, interesting) data, and having the information at our fingertips to deflect accusations that our system is down, slow, ugly, or whatever.

Assuming we enjoy monitoring as a discipline, and find it exciting to learn about different types of systems and ways they operate, their failure modes and all their peculiarities, we are going to want to share the same level of insight with our coworkers as we did for yourselves.

Inevitably, we'll find ourselves answering The Four Questions. These are questions which—for reasons that will become apparent—we never really had to ask when we were doing it on our own. The four questions of monitoring are:

- **Why did I get an alert?**
  The person is not asking, "Why did this alert trigger at this time?" They are asking why they got the alert at all.
- **Why didn't I get an alert?**
  Something happened that the owner of the system felt should have triggered an alert, but they didn't receive one.
- **What is being monitored on my system?**
  What reports and data can be pulled for their system (and in what form) so they can look at trending, performance, and forensic information after a failure.
- **What will alert on my system?**
  I'd like to be able to predict the conditions under which I will receive an alert for this system.

But wait! There's a fifth Beatle, I mean question.

- **<u>What do you monitor "standard?"</u>**
  What metrics and data are typically collected for systems like this? This is the inevitable (and logical) response when you say, "We put standard monitoring in place."

In the following chapters, I'm going to dig into each of these questions and explore why they get asked, how they ought to be answered, and how we can effectively prepare for them in advance.

But the takeaway I want to hold onto right now is this: When we decide to take on the role of monitoring engineer, these questions will be asked. Anticipate and look forward to these moments, because it means the person you're talking to is interested rather than apathetic. Rather than filling us with dread, let it inform our choices. If someone questions our knowledge, be comforted by the fact that every inquiry is an opportunity to teach and share. Recognize that if our colleagues are asking us questions, they view us as an expert.

Question One: Why Did I Get This Alert?

It's 8:45 am, you are just settling in at your desk, and you notice that one email came in overnight from your company's 24/7 operations desk. It says:

```
"We got an alert for high CPU on the server
WinSrvABC123 at 2:37 am. We didn't notice anything
when we jumped on the box. Can you explain what
happened?"
```

This is the easiest of all the four questions of monitoring for you to answer, if you have done your homework and set up your environment.

Before I dig in, I want to clarify that this is not the same question as, "What will alert on my server?" or "What are the monitoring and alerting standards for this type of device?" (I'll cover both of those later.) In this case, we're dealing strictly with a user's reaction after they receive an alert.

I also need to stress that it is imperative that you always take the time to answer this question, no matter how many times it's asked. It can be annoying, tedious, and time-consuming, but if you don't, all alerts will be dismissed as "useless" after a while. And that is the first step on a long road that leads to a CIO-mandated RFP for monitoring tools, being forced to defend your choice of solutions, and other conversations that are significantly more annoying, tedious, and time-consuming.

However, if you follow my tips below, the answer to this question should be more or less self-evident within the alert itself, and thus cut down on the number of times you will be asked in the first place.

The Story Before the Story

At the heart of the Pesach, or Passover, meal, there's a section called the Maggid ("to tell") where the reasons for this meal and the holiday are described. It contains the oldest text of the seder, and indeed, one of the oldest texts found in the Torah. It reads:

אֲרַמִּי אֹבֵד אָבִי
arami oved avi

Translated, this reads "My father was a wandering Aramean."

This sentence doesn't speak to the exodus from Mitzrayim, nor does it address the plagues which preceded the exodus. or the burning bush, or the years of enslavement. In this passage, the wandering Aramean is Yaakov (Jacob). His son Yosef (Joseph) is sold into slavery and sent down to Mitzrayim, where a chain of events results in him eventually becoming second-in-command to Paro (Pharaoh) and helping avert a region-wide famine. Yosef brings his entire family down to Mitzrayim to weather this seven-year event, but they become entrenched there and eventually Yaakov's entire family, also known as B'nei Yisrael (the House of Israel), become slaves to Paro. This condition–being slaves in Mitzrayim–is where the exodus story picks up the thread.

In essence, the Maggid begins at the story before the story before the story.

It's important to understand that the Maggid doesn't start with, "My father was a wandering Aramean..." That phrase appears only after the four questions I mentioned in the last chapter. The youngest person at the table asks, "Why is this all happening," and everyone sort of huddles up and starts to answer.

One of the lessons the Maggid is subtly conveying is this: When we're asked a question, we need to know how to provide context to the answer, or else the answer will be ignored.

> For many monitoring engineers, "Why did I get this alert?" is the first monitoring-related question they must answer. More important, it may be the first serious monitoring-related question a colleague may ask us. It's imperative that we not miss this invitation. We must also be prepared to respond in a way that answers the question and provides context so that the answer can be fully understood.

First, let's be clear: Monitoring is not alerting. Some people confuse getting a ticket, page, email, or other alert with actual monitoring. Monitoring is nothing more–and nothing less–than the ongoing collection of data about a particular element or set of elements. Alerting is a happy by-product of monitoring, because once you have metrics you can notify people when a specific metric is above or below a threshold. I mention this here, in connection with the first question, because customers sometimes ask (or demand) that you fix (or even turn off) "monitoring." What they really want is for you to change something about the alert they received, such as the frequency or level of detail. Rarely do they really mean you should stop collecting metrics.

To answer this question correctly, the bulk of your work is going to be focused on discovering the way an alert message was created. This is because the vagueness of the message is likely the reason why the recipient is confused. Basically, you should ensure that every alert message contains a few key pieces of information. The following are a few obvious ones:

- Name of the system that is experiencing the problem
- Specific component or sub-element that is experiencing the problem
- Current statistic or status of the sub-element
- Time the event occurred
- Time the alert was sent

The following is a good example:
```
FastEthernet 3 on Floor3Switch is down at 1:37 pm.
(alert sent 1:43 pm)
```

Some are slightly less obvious, but no less important:
- Any other identifying information about the device
- Any custom properties, indicating location, owner group, etc.
- OS type and version
- IP address
- DNS name or Sysname variables (if your device names are less than standard)
- The threshold value that breached and caused the alert
- The duration of the alert, i.e. how long it has been in effect
- A link or other reference to a place where the alert recipient can see this metric. This could take the form of:
- Device details
- Metric details, i.e. CPU average
- A report that shows this device (or a collection of devices where this is one member) and the metric involved

Finally, one element that should always be included in each alert:
- The name of alert

For straightforward alerts, this should not be a difficult task and can be something you should be able to copy and paste from one alert to another. The following is an example for a CPU alert. You can guess what each of the variables do.

```
CPU Utilization on the ${MachineType} device owned
by ${OwnerGroup} named ${NodeName} (IP:
${IP_Address}, DNS: ${DNS}) has been over
${CPU_Threshold} for more than 15 minutes. Current
load at ${AlertTriggerTime} is ${CPULoad}.
View full device details here: ${NodeDetailsURL}.
Click here to acknowledge the alert:
${AcknowledgeURL}
This message was brought to you by the alert:
${AlertName}
```

Yes, this creates more work when you are setting up the alert. But having an alert with this kind of messaging means that the recipient can more easily answer the question, "Why did I get this alert?"

For example:

- They have everything they need to identify the machine. The know which team owns it, what version of OS it's running, and the office or data center in which it is located.
- They have what they need to connect to the device, including name, DNS name, IP address, etc.
- They know what metric triggered the alert.
- They know when the problem was detected (because, let's face it, sometimes emails and get delayed).
- They have a way to quickly get to a status screen, which allows them to see the history of that metric and hopefully where the spike occurred.
- Finally, by including the ${AlertName}, you're enabling the recipient to help you help them. If they received a false alarm, they (and you) now know precisely which alert to research.

There is one more value you might want to include if you have a larger environment, and that's the name of the monitoring server (sometimes called a polling engine, management server, or collector). There are times when a device is moved to the wrong monitoring server (wrong because of networking rules, AD membership, DMZ boundaries, etc.). Having the name of the monitoring server in the message is a good sanity check in this situation.

If you do it right, which means solid documentation and providing information in meetings, then users — especially those in heavy support roles — will learn to analyze alerts on their own.

But what about the times when they still aren't sure why an alert came in? What then?

First, be prepared to test your alert. Of course, testing is something you should do every time you're ready to release a new alert into your environment, so the testing process should not be a challenge. Also, remember that sometimes you test everything but then the situation on the ground changes.

So, what do I mean when I say test your alert?

- Make a copy of the alert. Never test a live, normal production alert. Most monitoring tools have a COPY button in the alert manager for that very reason.
- Change the copy of the alert by adding an alert trigger for just one machine in question. (i.e. "where machine name is equal to WinSRVABC123").
- Set your triggering criteria (such as "CPULoad > 90%" or whatever) to a value low enough that it's guaranteed to trigger.

At that point, test the heck out of that sucker until both you and the recipient are satisfied that it works as expected. Copy whatever modifications you need over to the production copy of the alert and beware that updating the alert trigger may cause any existing alerts to re-fire. This means you might need to hold off on those changes until a relatively quiet moment.

The Prozac Moment

If you have worked in IT for more than ten minutes, you know that things go wrong. In fact, it should be obvious that we have jobs in IT specifically because things go wrong.

This is what systems monitoring and automation is all about: building solutions that automatically mind the shop, raise a flag when things start going south, and provide the information that helps us understand what happened and when. We transform this knowledge into a solution that both fixes the issue and improves the environment so that the same issue can be avoided in the future.

That's regular monitoring, though, and this chapter is about monitoring grief.

Let's talk about regular grief first. Grief is what my wife feels when dinner isn't ready because I got distracted watching cat videos and didn't put the casserole in the oven like she asked. Grief is what you feel when you are driving around at 3:00 am looking for an open convenience store because you didn't buy diapers earlier, like you said you would. Grief is what my mechanic feels when I tell him the "check engine" light has been on for the last two months.

Now, monitoring grief is what the monitoring engineer feels when consumers of monitoring — the network team, server admins, NOC operators, etc. — do things that cause problems down the road even when they know better. You — the monitoring engineer — have warned these people that certain actions will cause problems down the road, yet they choose to do them anyway.

I have spent the past two decades implementing monitoring systems at companies of all sizes. In that time, I've had the opportunity to witness certain behaviors that I eventually categorized into five, often sequential, stages. Organizations tend to experience these stages when rolling out a new monitoring system, but they also occur when a group or department starts to seriously implement an existing solution, when new capabilities are added to the current monitoring suite, or when it's Tuesday.

Spoiler alert: Unlike the standard Kubler-Ross model, acceptance is not on this list.

Stage One: Alert on Everything

This is the initial monitoring non-decision, a response to the simple, innocent question, "What do you want to be notified about?" The choice, a favorite of managers and teams who won't actually get the ticket (or email or page), is to set up monitoring using the wide-open firehose method. This choice is also frequently made by admins with a hair-on-fire problem in progress. This decision assumes that all the information is good information, and that they can "tune it down" once they see what's out there.

Stage Two: The Prozac Moment

After Stage One, the recipient of 734 emails in five minutes exclaims, "All these things can't possibly be going wrong!" While they are correct in principle, it ignores the fact that the computer can only define "going wrong" as specifically as the humans who requested the monitors in the first place.

I actually had to point out the following to someone I was working with.

"Bob, you insisted the system should alert you when the word "error" appears in the logfile. I'm not the one who forgot that "No error to report" was a return code."

Once Bob and I got down to the real issue, I went back to the monitoring tool and ratcheted things down to reasonable levels. But, when you do this, it is likely that "too much" will still show red, prompting a consumer to exclaim, "All these things can't possibly be going wrong!"

Worse, because the monitoring system was "wrong" before, monitoring must be wrong again.
Except this time, it isn't wrong. It's catching all the stuff that's been going up and down for weeks, months, or years without anyone noticing. Usually they were "fixed" by something tangential (such as someone rebooting the server for another reason), or masked by built-in service restarts. Perhaps users never complained, or maybe someone somewhere was jumping in and fixing it before anybody else knew about it.

The Prozac mentioned in this stage is what you wish you could give the system owner, to help them calm down, chill out, and realize that knowing about outages is the first step to avoiding them in the future.

But, of course, that's not what they want to do. In a moment of panicky insight, they are having a dawning realization that something is rotten in the data center, and it might have their name on it. So, they ask you to do the following.

Stage Three: Paint the Roses Green

Too many things are showing "down" and no amount of tweaking the monitoring is making them show "up" (because, ahem, they are down).

But, in a fit of stubborn pride, the system owner says, "They're not DOWN down, they're just, you know, a little down-ish right now." (This is an exact quote by a colleague, by the way.) And so, they demand that the monitoring engineer do whatever it takes to show those systems as up/good/green.

Whatever it takes, and I mean anything. Changing alert thresholds to impossible levels, such as only alerting if the system has been down for 30 hours, or a full week; disabling alerts entirely; and, in one case, under the threat of losing my job, creating a completely false page with blinking gifs of status dots that I had to re-color from red to green to show senior management.

What makes this stage even more ridiculous is that the work it takes to paint the roses green is usually more difficult and time-consuming than the work it takes to actually fix the issue.

But maybe I'm the only one who sees that. Or, at least until the organization finally stumbles upon Stage Four.

Stage Four: An Inconvenient Truth

The deceit of Stage Three goes on, sometimes for weeks or months, until something happens that cannot be covered up (or Photoshopped). At that point, the monitoring team (that's you) and the requestor find yourselves on a Service Restoration Team (SRT) phone call. Joining you on the call are about a dozen other engineers and a few high-ranking IT staffers, including the Chief Information Officer (CIO). The CIO joins all SRT meetings because they usually signal that a critical failure is impacting the business, or because the CIO just read The Phoenix Project, or because the CIO's boss demanded it, or all of the above.

Everyone is there to do exactly one thing: restore service as quickly as possible. Once that feat has been accomplished, they will perform a post-mortem analysis to find out what happened.

When the system goes down (or becomes severely impacted), everything is analyzed, checked, and restarted in real-time. At this point, a system owner who has developed a habit of buying green paint by the tanker-full has nowhere left to run or hide.

Now, the system's historical performance data is pulled and analyzed. In this hypothetical, the system has been down for a month and a half, even though it showed as being "up" in the reports. This is precisely where a simple, handmade gif is not going to cut it.

The truth comes out, in the form of reports, database dumps, and real-time test results.

If the system's owners manage to hold onto their jobs after this stage, they learn their lesson and set up monitoring the way it's supposed to be done. Right? Sadly, no. Instead, they usually enter Stage Five.

Stage Five: Gaming the System

The requester keeps you at arm's length as much as possible. The less sophisticated folks will find ways to monitor without all the messy inconvenience of setting up and managing a proper monitoring system. One thing these people do is keep tickets open so that new events don't trigger new tickets. Or they will give you fake email/pager information so that alerts go into the bit bucket. Or, they could put in a request to have monitoring turned off because it's "no longer necessary."

People who have been around for a while will request detailed information on exactly what permissions you need to monitor. That information is passed along to an (inevitably brand-new) security audit team, who could flat out deny the request because the permissions are too risky to give out.

Now, you have a choice. You can either pull out all your documentation and insist on receiving the previously agreed upon permissions, or go find another group that actually wants a solid monitoring.

What about this requester? The one who started off by saying, "Monitor everything" back in Stage One? Don't worry, he'll likely be back after the next system outage.

To give you more grief.

Question Two: Why DIDN'T I Get An Alert?

It's 9:45 am. Your first caller wanted to know why they got a particular alert, and you have just gotten off the phone with them. You can finally settle in and review the list of system improvements you planned on getting started today.

Then an email comes in. You click over to see what it is.

```
"We had an outage on CorpSRV042, but never got a
notification from your system. What exactly are we
paying all that money on a monitoring system for,
anyway?"
```

Of the Four Questions of Monitoring, this question is possibly the most labor intensive one to answer. This is because proving why something didn't trigger requires an intimate knowledge of the monitoring that is in place as well as the on-the-ground conditions of the system in question.

Unlike your first question of the day, there is not much you can do with this issue in terms of preparation to help lessen the work of finding a solution. For that reason, my advice is going to be a checklist of items and areas to look into.

I'm also going to be working on the assumption that an event really did happen, and that a monitor, which ostensibly should have caught it, was in place.

So, what could have failed?

What We Have Here is…

Option One: It's a non-failure failure that was designed to work that way

These types of failures generally occur because the device owner lacks awareness about how monitoring works. Once you narrow down the alleged "miss" to one of these, the next thing you need to evaluate is whether you should provide additional end-user education. This information can be shared in the form of lunch-and-learns, documentation, a narrated interpretive dance piece held in the cafeteria, etc.

Alert Windows
Some alerting systems will allow you to specify that the alert should only trigger during certain times of the day. If the problem occurred and corrected itself (or was manually corrected) outside of that window, then no alert would have been triggered.

Alert Duration
The best alerts are set up to look for more than one occurrence of the issue. Nobody wants to get a page at 2:00 am when a device failed one ping. But if you have an alert that is set to trigger when ping fails for 15 minutes, 13 minutes can seem like an eternity to the application support team that already knows the app is down.

The Alert Never Reset
There are many reasons why an alert never resets. Most of them are a result of human, rather than systemic, error. These include the following:

After the last failure (three weeks ago), the owners of the device worked on the problem. Unfortunately, they never actually got it to where your monitoring solution registered that it was actually resolved.

The team decided to close the ticket assuming it was probably nothing without bothering to look at the system.

The reset logic looks for a situation better than the trigger logic. A good example of this is illustrated by a disk alert that triggers when the disk is over 90 percent utilized, but doesn't reset until it's under 70 percent utilized. The team may clear logs and get things down to a nice, comfy 80 percent, but the alert never resets. That means that when the disk fills to 100 percent a week later, no alert is cut.

The device was unmanaged, quiesced, or otherwise in "don't collect data" mode.

 It's surprisingly easy to overlook that cute indicator, especially if your team does not make a habit of looking at the monitoring portal except when an alert directs them to a specific page. Or maybe your monitoring solution doesn't use a cute little indicator. Nevertheless, if your monitoring solution has the ability to stop collecting metrics for a device or sub-component, no alerts will trigger. Moreover, if you don't set up reports to show which devices are in this state (perhaps "...for more than X number of days"), teams may never realize (or more accurately, remember) that the system is suspiciously silent.

Mute, Squelch, Hush, or Please-Shut-Up-Now Functions
While different monitoring solutions handle this differently, the upshot is that "un-manage" stops all monitoring on the system, while "mute" will keep monitoring going, but turn off the alerting associated with a breached threshold. With that said, you'll need a way for teams to know when a system has been in this state for an extended period of time.

Parent-Child Part One
The first kind of parent-child option I want to talk about is the where a device, element, application, component, group, or "thingy" (I hope I don't lose you with these technical terms) is identified as the parent of another device, element, application, component, etc. The goal is to suppress downstream events because, typically, if the router is down, you don't want system down alerts for the switches connected to the router, or the servers connected to the switches. The correct state for downstream systems is "unreachable."

Parent-Child Part Two

The second kind of suppression is implicit but often unrecognized by many users. In its simplest terms, if a device is down, you won't get an alert about the disk being full. That makes sense, of course. But frequently, an application team will ask why they didn't get an alert that their app is down, and the reason is that the entire device was down during that same period.

Failure with Change Control

In this section, the issue that we're looking at changes either in the environment or within the monitoring system, which would cause an alert to be missed. I'm calling this "change control" because, if there had been a record or some other form of awareness of the change in question (as well as how the alert is configured), the device owner would probably not be calling you.

A credential changed

If someone changes one of the basic credentials for monitoring your monitoring tool ceases to be able to collect data. Usually you'll get some type of indication that this has happened, but not always. Sometimes the solution simply stops receiving data without making a peep.

The network changed

Sometimes the difference between beautiful data and total radio silence is one internal firewall rule or routing change. The problem is that the most basic monitoring — ping — is often not impacted, which means you don't get that "device down" message that tells everyone that something is amiss. Higher-level protocols like SNMP or WMI are suddenly blocked, leaving you with a device that is up (ping) with no disk or CPU information being collected.

A custom property changed

Modern monitoring solutions allow for custom fields, or properties, for things like owner group, location, environment (prod, dev, QA, etc.), server status (build, testing, managed), criticality (low, normal, business-critical) and more. Sophisticated alert triggers leverage these properties to provide escalated alerts for some machines, and simple warnings (or nothing) for others. But what happens when someone changes a server status from PRODUCTION to DEV? An alert won't trigger if it's configured to only trigger for PROD servers.

The monitored element has been removed or changed

This seems to happen most often with disk drives. Most environments have a "disk full" alert, but you'd be amazed at how many don't have one for "disk down/missing." Volumes can be unmounted or mounted with a new name with amazing frequency. When that happens, many monitoring tools do not automatically start monitoring the new element, and the tools that do almost never apply all the correct settings (like the custom properties I just mentioned). You end up with a situation where the device owner is completely aware of the update (since they set it up), while monitoring is left in the dark.

The server vanished into the virtualization horizon

The shift toward virtualization has been strong for over a decade now. Over the past three years, the drive to cloud has been even stronger. When a server goes from physical to virtual, it's effectively a whole new machine. Even though the IP address and server name are the same, the drives go from a series of physical disks attached to a real storage controller to (usually fewer) volumes that appear to be running off a generic SCSI bus. Not only that, but the nature of the other elements (interfaces, hardware monitors, CPU, and more) all completely change. Almost all monitoring tools require manual updating to account for those changes, or else you are left with ghost elements that don't respond to polling requests. Moving a business service to the cloud is often even more extreme. As with physical-to-virtual migrations, even in the case of a "lift and shift" operation, where the name of the server, its DNS entry, and (sometimes) even its IP address remain the same, the fundamental nature of cloud-based architecture means that everything you once monitored now has little relevance to the reality of that system. The specifics of what is important to monitor on a virtual or cloud-based entity are beyond the scope of this book. The point I'm making here is that, if the monitoring team doesn't know the shift is happening, you may be monitoring irrelevant elements, if they exist at all.

Failure of the Monitoring Technology

The previous two sections speak to educational or procedural breakdowns. But loath as I am to admit it, sometimes our monitoring tools fail us, too:

The element or device is not actually getting polled
Often, this is a result of disks or other elements being removed and added, or it could be a P-to-V migration (see previous section). But it also happens that an element simply stops getting polled. You'll see this when you dig into the detailed data and find that no data has been collected for a specific period of time.

The agent has stopped working
Monitoring agents are both the strength and the Achilles heel of some solutions. On the one hand, they can collect massive amounts of data and act almost instantaneously to respond to errors. On the downside, they require an additional layer of process and management to ensure they haven't failed (or been disabled by well-meaning but uninformed support staff).

Polling interval is throttled
Sometimes polling servers get overwhelmed by the volume of data they are being asked to collect. One of the first things a good polling server does, in this situation, is pull back on polling cycles so that it can collect at least some data from each element rather than simply going belly-up. You can see this in the monitoring system as gaps in data sets. It's not a wholesale loss of polling, but sort of a herky-jerky collection. Because of that, alerts fail to trigger because the data is simply not collected.

Polling data is out of sync
This one can be quite challenging to nail down. In some cases, a monitoring system will add data into the central data store using localized times, either from the polling engine or from the target device itself. If that happens, an event that occurred at 9:00 am in New York shows up as having happened at 8:00 am in Chicago. This shouldn't be a problem unless, as mentioned earlier, you have an alerting window that won't trigger an alert before 9:00 am.

Failure Somewhere After the Monitoring Solution

It may be a bitter pill to swallow, but we have to recognize that, at least sometimes, monitoring isn't the center of the universe. If everything within your monitoring solution checks out and you are still scratching your head, here are some other possibilities to explore:

Email, or whatever notification system you use, is down

One of the most obvious yet overlooked areas to check is the system that sends out alerts. If your email is down, you won't get the email that tells you your email server has crashed.

Event correlation rules

Event correlation rules are wonderful, magical things. They take you beyond the simple parent-child suppression discussed earlier, and into a whole new realm of dependencies. But there are times when they inhibit a good alert in an unexpected way, including:

De-duplication

The point of de-duplication is to keep multiple alerts from creating multiple tickets. But if a ticket closed and didn't update the event correlation system, de-dup will continue forever.

Blackout/Maintenance windows

Another common feature for EC systems is the ability to look up a separate data source that lists times when a device is "out of service." This can be a recurring schedule, or a specific one-time rule. Either way, you'll want to check if the device in question was listed on the blackout list when the error occurred.

Already open ticket

Ticket systems can be quite sophisticated, and many have the ability to suppress new tickets if there is already one open for the same alert/device combination. If you have a team that forgets to close their old ticket, they may never hear about the new events.

Hokey Religions Are No Match For a Good Blaster, Kid

After laying out all the potential ways that monitoring can be missed, it is only fair to give you some advice on techniques or tools you can use to identify, resolve, or altogether avoid these problems.

An Ounce of Prevention

Here are some things to have in place that will let you know when all is not puppy dogs and rainbows:

Alerts that give you a view of the health of your environment
Under the heading of "who watches the watchmen," any moderately sophisticated or mission-critical monitoring environment should have internal and external checks to help ensure that things are working well. These include:

A non-critical alert that notifies the monitoring team if data has not been collected for a specific node in X minutes.
A non-critical alert that notifies when a polling server/collector hasn't written any data to the database in X minutes.
Treating your monitoring solution like an application that needs monitoring, because, you know, it does! The trick is to make the case, usually to the bean counters, that you can't do this from the monitoring solution itself. Either have a second instance of the same tool, or use another solution, including open source.

Have a way to test individual aspects of the alert stream
You know that awful, sinking feeling you get when you realize that no alerts have been going out because one piece of the alerting infrastructure failed on you? I know. No fun. To avoid this, start by understanding and documenting every step an alert takes, from the source device through to the ticket, email, page, or smoke signal that is sent to the alert recipient. From there, create and document the ways you can validate that each of those steps is working independently. This will allow you to quickly validate each subsystem and nail down the point at which a message may have gotten lost.

Wait. You can test each alert subsystem?

A test procedure is just a monitor waiting for your loving touch. Get it done. You'll need to do it on a separate system since, you know, if your alerting infrastructure is broken you won't get an alert. This can usually be done inexpensively. Just to be clear, once you can manually test each of your alert infrastructure components (monitoring, event correlation, etc.), turn those manual tests into continuous monitors, and then set those monitors up with thresholds to ensure you get an alert.

Create a deadman switch

The concept is that you get an alert if something doesn't happen. First set up an event which triggers an alert that goes all the way through the system regularly. Then set up another monitor to alert when the first message has not been seen in X minutes.

Now, About That Pound of Cure

Inevitably, you'll have to dig in and analyze a failed alert. As mentioned earlier, the problem might be that the device has changed. It could be a new firewall rule, an SNMP string change, or the agent on the target device died. It could have gotten stuck in your correlation rules or the ticket queue. If that's the case, any of the earlier sections of this chapter have pointed you toward the problem, so the solution will be self-evident. If that doesn't do the trick, here are some specific techniques to use.

Re-scan the device

Some solutions have a "test" or "rescan" option. Some will permit you to run that command through an API, making the process even more programmatic. The point is to re-discover the sub-elements on the device and see what happens. Usually this process will fail and point to the error that requires a fix.

Re-add the device

If re-scanning the device doesn't do it, try to re-add it as a new device. Once again, if there's a problem with this specific device (or class of device) then the failure you receive will point you toward the thing you need to fix.

Test the alert

Are you sure your logic was solid? Be prepared to copy the alert and add a statement limiting it down to the single device in question. Then re-fire that sucker and see if it flies.

When a Question Shouldn't Be Answered

The following thoughts were generously shared with me by Rabbi Raphael Davidovich. You can find more of his ideas over on his blog: https://thisshiurisaboutyou.wordpress.com/

אֵיכָה | יָשְׁבָה בָדָד
Eicha yashva badad

"How does the city sit alone, that was once full of people?"

This quote from the book of Eicha (Lamentations) Chapter One, Verse One, has as its introductory word Eicha, which translates to "How?" However, unlike the English word how, which has a real meaning and a rhetorical meaning, the word Eicha seems to only be used in the rhetorical sense, meaning, no actual answer is expected. To answer the question would be out of place, a faux pas of sorts.

The book is read in shuls every year on the night of Tisha B'Av, the ninth day of the Hebrew month of Av, which commemorates the destruction of the Temple in Jerusalem. Yet rarely has an opening word meant so much. The rabbis and poets who composed and formulated the readings of this day ran with the theme introduced by this word.

First of all, they made sure that the word Eicha would also be read on the Shabbos preceding the fast day in the Torah portion for that week (Deut. 1:12) and the reading from the prophets (Isaiah 1:21.)

They certainly followed Yirmiyahu (Jeremiah)'s lead in deciding that the word was so potent that it wouldn't suffice as the mere opening word of chapter one, but was to be repeated as the opening word of chapters two and four, out of five chapters.

The various authors of the later Kinos (lamentation poems) would end up using the word dozens if not hundreds of times in the course of their poetry. What is so meaningful about this rhetorical flourish that made it the linguistic linchpin of the day?

As the day deals with pain and suffering in its various forms, the rhetorical "How?" never answered, is never meant to be answered in a direct intellectual way. This is in line with the teaching from Pirkei Avos (Teachings of our Fathers) 4:23, which says, "Do not appease your fellow in the time of his anger; do not console him while his dead lies before him…" When someone is suffering, he may ask questions. But those questions are not meant to be answered. They are exclamations of pain, and no attempt should be made in the heat of the pain to resolve it through conventional tools of appeasement or consolation. In the immediacy of loss, there are no good answers.

This idea, embodied in this word, has come to define Tisha B'Av, and through it has defined the nature of the afflicted person's questions. They aren't questions. They are "questions." I often apply insights of this nature to human relationships. In this case, the eicha can sometimes be translated to "Why?" as in, "Why is this happening to me?" It's always a good idea to know if the question is meant rhetorically or inquisitively. And as the Eicha is never answered in a straightforward manner in these biblical examples, or in the centuries of rabbinic poetry that followed, it's always the safest and wisest bet to assume that it's meant rhetorically, and then to respond in kind. If you misjudged, and the one person in a thousand meant for you to answer, I'm sure he will be glad to clarify, and you will have made the error of being too sensitive; not a bad idea. On the other hand, if you answer a rhetorical cry of anguish with an intellectual response, you may very well be assumed to be a monster. Easy bet, great odds.

Another application of this lesson in rhetorical language that does not use the word Eicha can be found in a passage in the Haggadah. The Haggadah is famous for its depiction of four sons who ask questions, and the suggested replies to those questions. The questions of the wise and simple sons speak for themselves. The wise question is elaborate and wordy, speaking of multiple layers of legal material. The simple son's question is, well, simple: "What's this?"

But the second question listed seems to get a lot of flak it doesn't deserve. "What is this service/work to you?" does not seem particularly egregious. What's more, the Haggadah's suggested answer is not the answer that the Torah itself offers to said question. If you don't believe me, look it up, in Shemot (Exodus) 12:26-27.In fact, in an oft-missed quote, the Haggadah text uses the Torah's answer (verse 27) to the wicked son later on, in its answer to the question, "The Passover that our ancestors ate when the Temple stood; what is it for?"

Some have suggested that the offense emerges from the word "service," which implies that Passover is work. Yet the answer doesn't hold, since the line preceding the question inoffensively describes the ritual as Avoda, or service/work.

Yet others find the rudeness in the word Lachem ("to you"). This seems to be the fault that the Haggadah finds in the question. "To you" and not " to him." He excludes himself from the community. I won't deny that this is the Haggadah's angle, yet it doesn't suffice as the sole cause of offense. The wise son's question also uses the "to you" in its phrasing. And given that the Torah is saying that a later generation will ask the present generation about the Torah and its commandments, it only makes sense that they are addressing them in the second person.

The offense is to be found in the combination of the "to you" together with the way that the Torah introduces the children's statement. Take a look at verse 26. "And it will be when your children tell you, 'What is this work to you?'" Compare it to the other questions that are introduced by, "When your son asks you…" Here, the sons will tell, not ask, you, not ask. Sometimes, a statement might have a question mark appended to its ending, but it is not a question.

A statement can have a question embedded in it; a question that should be answered. And in fact, the Torah does answer this question. But the rabbis who wrote the text of the Haggadah saw another layer of meaning here, a meaning in which questions come with attitude. And while the question needs to be answered, perhaps later, the tone needs to be addressed in its own statement.

This brings to my mind a frequent occurrence with one of my rabbis in Yeshiva. While giving a lecture, he would interpret a multi-layered passage that might involve a multi-layered citation. He would explain how a 13th-century rabbi was disagreeing with an 11th-century rabbi who was explaining a Talmudic passage from the 4th century. A student would call out that he didn't accept or understand something in the presentation. The lecturing rabbi would then reply, "Who is your problem with? Me, or the 13th-century rabbi, or the 11th-century rabbi, or the Talmudic passage?" He forced the student to see the many possible layers of the question, in order to refine the problem. Our Haggadah's skeptic son has to be answered on every level; the emotional chutzpa (brash) level as well as the factual level.

****

People who pursue a career in technical fields, especially but not exclusively the discipline of monitoring, can find a few takeaways in all of this.

First, we need to learn to recognize when a colleague is asking Eicha (the emotional how, as Rabbi Davidovich explained) versus the intellectual how. We also need to learn to respond in kind. Empathy is a skill everyone, from the CEO on down, needs to learn, practice, and foster. When an application owner is still wrapping their head around a major outage and asks, "How the hell did this happen?" understand that this is not the time to offer a detailed technical analysis.

Second, but closely related, is to begin to build a catalogue of effective ways to respond to an Eicha question. Repeating the verse from Pirkei Avos that Rabbi Davidovich quoted earlier, "Do not appease your fellow in the time of his anger; do not console him while his dead lies before him." Okay, that's what not to do. But what should we do? As a monitoring professional, it's a sure thing you will be faced with colleagues who are struggling emotionally with an event that your tools alerted them to. Building a repertoire of responses, from supportive silence to non-committal words of comfort, will be critical to helping them move past the momentary anguish and on to the work of solving the issue.

Finally, as we learned about the question from the Skeptical child, we need to learn to listen for tone as well as content. Part of our work is separating tone from content, so we can ignore a prickly personality and focus on answering the heart of the question. But the opposite is also true; we need to address belligerence before it gets out of hand, before people mistakenly believe that we're a willing doormat for their emotional abuse.

Question Three: What is Being Monitored On My System?

It's 1:35 pm. Your first two callers — the first, who wanted to know why they got a particular alert, and the second, who wanted to know why they didn't get an alert — are finally a distant memory. You've managed to squeeze in some productive work setting up a monitor that will detect when your WAN router's cellular backup circuit...

That's as far as you get into that thought before your manager ambles over and looks at you expectantly over the cube wall.

"I just met with the manager of the APP-X support team," he tells you. "They want a matrix of what is monitored on their system."

To his credit he adds, "I checked the reports section in the monitoring portal, but nothing jumped out at me. Did I overlook something?"

This question is solved with a combination of foresight (knowing you will be asked this question), preparation, and know-how.

It is also one of the questions where the steps are extremely specific to the monitoring solutions you are using. An agent-based solution may have a lot of this information embedded in the agent itself, information which may or may not need to be specifically requested and aggregated on a central machine. On the other hand, an agentless toolset will store that information in a centralized database or configuration system.

It's important to understand that this is a question that you can answer, and with some preparation you can have the answer with the push of a button or two. But like so many things in this book, preparation now will save you from desperation and sleep deprivation later.

It's also important to recognize that this type of report is absolutely essential, both to you and the systems owner. Not having this information usually results in repeated requests for monitors or alerts that are already in place. If the monitoring owners are on top of their game, they know that the monitoring is already there. But if this question can't be answered for monitoring consumers, it's easily forgotten or overlooked. The result is that the same monitor or alert is accidentally created again and again under different names or slightly different variations, resulting in a disorganized, frustrating, inefficient mess.

Have you ever seen a monitoring system with hundreds of alerts configured? If you aren't already experiencing this problem, you're likely dreading its inevitability. But if you are prepared for this question, it's neither inevitable nor something to fear.

Monitoring Philosophy

I believe strongly that monitoring is more than just watching elements and triggering alerts, whether those alerts result in tickets, emails, pager messages, or an ahoogah noise over the loudspeaker. The scope of your monitoring solution should cover all three pillars of observability (metrics, logs, and traces) in some form. Bear in mind, too, that monitoring is used not only for alerting, but also capacity planning, performance analysis, and forensics. For example, you may never alert on the size of the swap drive, but you will absolutely want to know what its size was during the time of a crash. You might never alert on a line of code that is consistently slowing down a transaction, but your developers will want to have that data available for code review. For that reason, knowing what is monitored is essential, even if you won't alert on some of those elements.

The Knee Bone's Connected to the…

Let's take a moment to break down the areas of monitoring data, which can include the following:

Hardware information for the device itself. Think of this part as the chassis or box, even if it's virtual. CPU and RAM are examples, as are administrator modules. The most important thing to remember is that you are only interested in hardware that applies to the unit as a whole, not sub-elements like cards, disks, ports, etc.

You may have one, more than one, or zero hardware sub-elements. Network cards, disks, external mount points, and VLANs are just a few examples of hardware sub-elements.

Specialized hardware elements include fans, power supplies, temperature sensors, and the like.

Specifics of virtualized elements running on top of the physical hardware, which include VM configurations and software defined switching components.

Those elements are just on-premises examples. The same exercise extends to your cloud-based infrastructure.

Your box in the sky, i.e. persistent servers, should be treated the same as their on-premises counterparts above.

For containers, you want to treat the orchestrator as the primary device, and each container as a sub-component.

Your cloud platform, which really functions as a single giant box, also needs to be monitored.

Finally, you move on to applications.

Start with application components, including services, processes, counters, logfile indicators, and more; these are all the things that make up a holistic view of an application.

Add to that synthetic user experience tests.

Finally, include application tracing if your tool or tools support it.

And then...

Actually, I'm going to stop here. While there are certainly many more items on that list, if you can master the concept of those first few bullets, adding more should come fairly easily. As I'm fond of saying, "Salt to taste."

It should be noted that this type of report is not a fire-and-forget affair. It's more like a labor of love that you will come back to and refine over time. And you'll need to, because this is not a question you're going to be asked once or twice and then never again. It's a report that teams will want regularly, quarterly at least, possibly more often.

Hello, It's Me Again

Let's get back to our original question. If you are able to quickly and conveniently answer it, you are on the fast track to perfecting what is, in my opinion, the single most important and yet under-performed task for a monitoring expert: checking with monitoring consumers to find out if the monitoring and alerting they are receiving is meeting their needs.

I know! Crazy, right?

Imagine how that conversation would go. If the monitoring consumer isn't really getting what they want, they'll still be blown away by the fact that you and your team are proactively checking in to see what's up. They'll therefore be much more amenable to the conversation that ensues, in which you can go back to the drawing board to get them monitoring that does meet their needs. Of course, if monitoring is doing well for them, coming back around to check just earns you extra brownie points.

Remember, though: this only works if you go to them with a clear list of how each of their systems is being monitored.

One Size Fits… Some?

I also need to point out that this will likely not be a one-report-fits-all-device-types solution. The report you create for network devices like routers and access points may need to be radically different from the one you build for server-type devices. Virtual hosts may need data points that have no relevance to anything else. Specialty devices like load balancers, UPS-es, or environmental systems are in a class of their own. Cloud? Containers? They're all going to require thoughtful consideration to expose the data that matters to you and to those benefiting from the monitoring you're providing.

This exercise will also highlight the areas where knowing the underlying hardware/hosts and applications is not only impossible, it's utterly unnecessary. If you are digging into an environment ruled by containers, orchestration, and elastic compute workloads, you not only won't know how many CPUs you're using, you shouldn't care. In those environments, the focus should be on what you know about the application, the interactions between services, etc.

Finally, to get what you want, you also have to understand how the monitoring data that uncovers all these elements are stored, and be extremely comfortable interacting with that system. The process to get this information is going to be specific to the monitoring toolset you are using.

As I mentioned earlier, this type of report is push-button simple on some toolsets. If that's the case for you, feel free to stop reading and walk away with the knowledge that you will be asked this question on a regular basis, and you should be prepared to push that button.

If it's not push-button simple, you're going to need to get creative. I cannot possibly offer you a specific set of actions that cover every monitoring solution on the market. What I can do is make the presumption that you're going to be working with a SQL-based database of some type (whether that's MS-SQL, MySQL, PostgreSQL, or something else), and offer some tricks that DBAs use and wish we weekend table-tinkerers knew.

SQL in the Buff

If you've never worked with SQL or databases before, I would say stop here, pick up a good book (my fellow SolarWinds® Head Geek™ Thomas LaRock recommends T-SQL Fundamentals by Itzik Ben-Gan, and that's as good a reference as you could hope for), and read that before continuing on.

Be Selective

Those new to SQL, or anyone used to working with smaller data sets, may not realize how much small syntax changes can affect overall performance.

As a rule, never use select * in any query that you are going to keep around for longer than five minutes. There's a very good likelihood it will not only impact performance, but have downstream consequences. Also, it's really lazy, and you don't want to be known as that developer, do you?

There's also the common misconception that select TOP 1 is more efficient than other select statements because it's only returning the first record. That's not true because the full query has to run (and ostensibly sort, because otherwise TOP 1 of what?) before the top records are known. Use MAX() instead. Once again, this only applies to queries you are going to keep, i.e. enshrine in production as a report, alert trigger, etc. If you are testing, have at it, but know that you need to optimize that sucker if it's going to last longer than five or ten minutes.

Learn to use a query plan tool. There's one built into SQL Management Studio, but there are other off- and online tools to help you out. That helps you understand the performance impact that your code is having, so that if you choose to run it every minute, you recognize and accept the effect it will have.

State of a Union

The broader the categories of elements you try to pull into a single report, the more likely it will be that you're going to need to add columns. For example, if you want to show wireless signal strength and bandwidth in the same report, you'd obviously have to include

- Radio type (A/B/G/N)
- Signal strength
- Interface type (ethernet, fast ethernet, gig ethernet, etc.)
- Interface speed
- Etc.

Throw in CPU, RAM, running time (for ephemeral containers) and such, and you can have a report that's pulling from 10 different sources, with little to match between them. This makes regular JOIN statements difficult and expensive.

However, you can run nearly independent queries against those tables and simply merge all the results together using a UNION command. That will make the resulting query much faster.

There's just one hitch. Each table has to have all the same columns.

One way to get around that is to add blank fields into all the table results, as needed. Therefore, when pulling the bandwidth info, I might say*:

```
Select
NodeID, NodeName, InterfaceName, InterfaceSpeed, '' as
Radio, '' as Signal
from Interfaces
UNION ALL
     NodeID, NodeName, '' as InterfaceName, '' as
InterfaceSpeed, Radio, Signal
     From Wireless
```

This query is simplified to show how to insert blank columns into a query. If your query actually looks like this, your DBA will probably hunt you down and offer to percussively improve your query writing skills.

A More Perfect Union

The technique above, however, will quickly lead to a result set with 300 columns. Nobody likes that.

So my suggestion is to make your columns a little more generic, and therefore multi-purpose:

```
Select
NodeID, NodeName, NIC as ElementType, InterfaceName as
Element, InterfaceDescription as Description,
InterfaceSpeed as Capacity
from Interfaces
UNION ALL
NodeID, NodeName, Wireless as ElementType, Radio as
Element, WirelessDescription as Description, Signal as
Capacity
        From Wireless
```

Doing this for all of the tables you're pulling from will allow you to create a result set that looks something like this.

statusled	nodeid	caption	LED	elementtype	element	Description		capacity
Up.gif	1	stp-aix71	Up.gif	CPU	CPU Count:		4	0
Up.gif	1	stp-aix71	Up.gif	RAM	Total RAM		8.32E+09	0
Up.gif	1	stp-aix71	Up.gif	NIC	ent1	Ethernet		1000000000
Up.gif	1	stp-aix71	Up.gif	DISK	/dev/fwdump	Fixed Disk		134217728
Up.gif	1	stp-aix71	Up.gif	DISK	/dev/hd1	Fixed Disk		5502926848
Up.gif	2	lab-aix53-ppc64	Up.gif	CPU	CPU Count:		1	0
Up.gif	4	VMAN-2008R2-IIS.vman.lab	Up.gif	CPU	CPU Count:		2	0
Up.gif	4	VMAN-2008R2-IIS.vman.lab	Up.gif	RAM	Total RAM		2.15E+09	0
Up.gif	4	VMAN-2008R2-IIS.vman.lab	Up.gif	NIC	Intel(R) PRO/1000 MT Network Connection	Ethernet		1000000000
Up.gif	4	VMAN-2008R2-IIS.vman.lab	Up.gif	DISK	C:\ Label: 583721ff	Fixed Disk		42842714112
Up.gif	4	VMAN-2008R2-IIS.vman.lab	Unknow	APP	Processor Queue Length	01UA_Windows_Standard		0
Up.gif	10	Tex-3750.aus.lab	Up.gif	CPU	CPU Count:		1	0
Up.gif	10	Tex-3750.aus.lab	Up.gif	RAM	Total RAM		1.33E+08	0
Up.gif	10	Tex-3750.aus.lab	Up	HW	CISCO2821	Fan (Up): Fan 1 (Up), Fan 2 (Up), Fan 3 (Up)		0
Up.gif	10	Tex-3750.aus.lab	Up.gif	NIC	GigabitEthernet0/0	Ethernet		1000000000

The only other trick is that you'll need to do some conversions to keep the capacity data types consistent. But otherwise, once the report is written, it becomes a simple matter to run for the entire environment or a subset.

The Sky's the Limit. Or Is It?

I could stop here, and you would have, more or less, the building blocks you need to build your own "What is Monitored on My System" report.

But there is one more piece that takes this type of report to the next level: thresholds.

Including the built-in thresholds for these elements increases complexity to the query, but also adds an entirely new and important dimension to the information you are providing. See the following results:

statusled	nodeid	caption	LED	elementtype	element	Description	capacity	threshold_value	warn	crit
Up.gif	1	stp-aix71	Up.gif	CPU	CPU Count:		4	0 CPU Utilization	80	90
Up.gif	1	stp-aix71	Up.gif	RAM	Total RAM		8.32E+09	0 RAM Utilization	80	90
Up.gif	1	stp-aix71	Up.gif	NIC	ent1	Ethernet	1000000000	bandwidth in/out	80/80	50/90
Up.gif	1	stp-aix71	Up.gif	DISK	/dev/fwdump	Fixed Disk	134217728			
Up.gif	4	VMAN-2008R2-IIS.vman.lab	Up.gif	CPU	CPU Count:		2	0 CPU Utilization	80	90
Up.gif	4	VMAN-2008R2-IIS.vman.lab	Up.gif	RAM	Total RAM		2.15E+09	0 RAM Utilization	80	90
Up.gif	4	VMAN-2008R2-IIS.vman.lab	Up.gif	NIC	Intel(R) PRO/1000 MT Network Connection	Ethernet	1000000000	bandwidth in/out	80/80	50/90
Up.gif	4	VMAN-2008R2-IIS.vman.lab	Up.gif	DISK	C:\ Label: 583721ff	Fixed Disk	42842714112			
Up.gif	8	LAB-NLB2012-02	Unknown	APP	Processor Queue Length	01UA_Windows_Standard		0 CPU Utilization	NULL	NULL
Up.gif	8	LAB-NLB2012-02	Up.gif	CPU	CPU Count:		2	0 CPU Utilization	80	90
Up.gif	8	LAB-NLB2012-02	Up.gif	RAM	Total RAM		2.97E+09	0 RAM Utilization	80	90
Up.gif	8	LAB-NLB2012-02	Up.gif	NIC	Microsoft Hyper-V Network Adapter	Ethernet	1000000000	bandwidth in/out	80/80	50/90
Up.gif	8	LAB-NLB2012-02	Up.gif	DISK	C:\ Label: EEBFA16E	Fixed Disk	42579521536			
Up.gif	8	LAB-NLB2012-02	Up	APP	Processor Queue Length	01UA_Windows_Standard		0 CPU Utilization	NULL	NULL
Up.gif	10	Tex-3750.aus.lab	Up.gif	CPU	CPU Count:		1	0 CPU Utilization	80	90
Up.gif	10	Tex-3750.aus.lab	Up.gif	RAM	Total RAM		1.33E+08	0 RAM Utilization	80	90
Up.gif	10	Tex-3750.aus.lab	Up.gif	NIC	GigabitEthernet0/0	Ethernet	1000000000	bandwidth in/out	80/80	50/90
Up.gif	10	Tex-3750.aus.lab	Up	HW	CISCO2821	Fan (Up): Fan 1 (Up), Fan 2 (Up), Fan 3 (Up)				
Up.gif	11	lab-mpls-pe-tex.lab.ew	Up.gif	CPU	CPU Count:		1	0 CPU Utilization	80	90
Up.gif	11	lab-mpls-pe-tex.lab.ew	Up.gif	RAM	Total RAM		7.11E+08	0 RAM Utilization	80	90
Up.gif	11	lab-mpls-pe-tex.lab.ew	Up.gif	NIC	FastEthernet0/0	Ethernet	100000000	bandwidth in/out	80/80	50/90
Up.gif	11	lab-mpls-pe-tex.lab.ew	Up.gif	NIC	FastEthernet0/0-mpls layer	MPLS	100000000	bandwidth in/out	80/80	50/90
Up.gif	11	lab-mpls-pe-tex.lab.ew	Up.gif	NIC	FastEthernet0/1	Ethernet	100000000	bandwidth in/out	80/80	50/90
Up.gif	11	lab-mpls-pe-tex.lab.ew	Up	HW	CISCO2811	Fan (Up): Fan 1 (Up), Fan 2 (Up), Fan 3 (Up)				

It's 90 Percent Perspiration

While answering this question requires persistence, skill, and an in-depth knowledge of your monitoring tool set, the benefits are significantly greater than for the previous two questions.

Done right, teams can use this report to validate that the correct elements on each device are monitored; nothing is left out and nothing that's been decommissioned is still there. And when an alert does trigger, it will be easier to understand where you can look for hints, instead of just clicking around screens looking for something interesting.

The 10 Plagues: Black Swans, Bolts from the Blue, and Other Unpredictable Effects

How do so many people know about the 10 plagues mentioned in the bible and be able to name at least a few? Possibly because movies like The Ten Commandments and Prince of Egypt, not to mention more modern productions, such as The Mummy and The Abominable Dr. Phibes, turned such occurrences into fixtures of pop culture.

Perhaps it's because those segments of the bible are so visceral, so iconic, that they stick with folks to such an extent that they know them without knowing how they know them.

But, in case you aren't one of those people, let's review.

After many years away, Moshe (Moses) returns to Mitzrayim (Egypt) and, along with his brother Aharon (Aaron), gains an audience with Paro (Pharaoh). Moshe demands that Paro release the Israelites, who have been enslaved for 230 years. Paro refuses, and sends them away. In the morning, as Paro is coming in from the Nile river, Moshe and Aharon face him, striking the river, as God commanded, so that the water turns to blood. While his magicians can replicate the "trick" of turning water to blood, they can't turn it back. Seven days later, Moshe and Aharon again confront Paro, asking him to release the Israelites or be plagued with frogs. Paro again refuses to let the slaves go and frogs swarm across the land. Paro's magicians are again able to produce frogs but can't remove them. And so Paro summons Moshe and Aharon and asks them to ask God to remove the frogs, and he'll release the Israelites. But after the frogs are gone, Paro reneges on his agreement. This pattern repeats, with slight variations, for the plague of lice, attacks of wild beasts, diseased livestock, boils, burning hail, locusts, a darkness that lasts three days, and finally the death of the firstborn child from every family. After this final plague, Paro finally relents and tells Moshe and Aharon that the Israelites are free to leave.

The plagues are disconcerting and powerful, whether you experience the story by watching it on a screen, in a graphic novel, or with nothing but the original language on a page. But, like everything else in the Haggadah, there's more to these narrative elements than appear on the surface.

The first thing I'll note is that, with the exception of the story of Noah and the Ark, no section of the Torah elicits as strong a reaction of pediatric theology as the plagues do. Pediatric theology happens when an otherwise educated adult–someone who can balance a checkbook, perform advanced math, and hold down a job–understands a section of religious text using knowledge they picked up in third grade Bible class. They reach a conclusion about it without studying it independently or giving it any deeper or further thought. These are people who understand that the poem, "Tiger, Tiger, Burning Bright" is not actually about a jungle cat on fire, but scoff at the idea that the waters of the Red Sea parted, and instead insist that it must have just been low tide. This, despite the fact that there are literally hundreds of books, written by authors over centuries of history, on that one topic alone. These adults, though, continue to behave as if what they learned in childhood is all there is to say on the subject.

Without digging into the specifics of each plague, I'll simply say that the actual descriptions defy scientific explanation, and that's okay. Not because God is an irrational magic person in the sky who changes the laws of physics to fit a personal whim, but because the actual descriptions of the plagues point us to far deeper understandings. Let's take the plague of choshech (darkness) as an example.

וַיֵּט מֹשֶׁה אֶת־יָדוֹ עַל־הַשָּׁמָיִם וַיְהִי חֹשֶׁךְ־אֲפֵלָה
בְּכָל־אֶרֶץ מִצְרַיִם שְׁלֹשֶׁת יָמִים
Vayet Moshe et-yado al-hashamayim vayehi choshech-afelah bechol-erets Mitsrayim shloshet yamim.

לֹא־רָאוּ אִישׁ אֶת־אָחִיו וְלֹא־קָמוּ אִישׁ מִתַּחְתָּיו שְׁלֹשֶׁת
יָמִים וּלְכָל־בְּנֵי יִשְׂרָאֵל הָיָה אוֹר בְּמוֹשְׁבֹתָם
Lo-ra'u ish et-achiv velo-kamu ish mitachtav shloshet yamim ulechol-beney Yisra'el hayah or bemoshevotam.

And so Moshe stretched forth his hand toward the heavens, and there was thick darkness over the entire land of Egypt for three days.
They did not see each other, and no one rose from his place for three days, but for all the children of Israel there was light in their dwellings.

The text is terse, but hints at something more than a lack of light. The Torah specifically says, "They did not see each other..." What? They had no candles? And, "...no one rose from his place for three days..." Not even for bathroom breaks? You'd think in a national blackout people would be running from house to house in panic. And most tellingly, "...but for all the children of Israel there was light in their dwellings." Because they had ancient night vision goggles?

To understand more, I'm going to turn to the commentary.

First up is Rabbi Shlomo Yitzchaki (more commonly known as Rashi, who lived in France from 1040-1105). About this plague he explained, "...no one rose from his place. If he was sitting, he was unable to stand, and if he was standing, he was unable to sit."

Next, I look to Rabbi Moses ben Maimon (also known as Rambam, 1135-1204), who said, "There was a great darkness which would descend upon them and which would extinguish every light, just as in all deep caverns and in all extremely dark places where light cannot exist as it is swallowed up in the density of thick darkness."

This is clearly not a normal darkness. But what is the Torah getting at? We have a sense of what is happening, but not such a clear understanding of why. To get to the heart of it, we need to examine the details more closely.

While many people note the fact that the darkness affected the Mitzrim (Egyptians) but not the Jews, a detail that is often overlooked is that the darkness lasted for just three days, rather than a week like most of the other plagues. Numbers given in the Torah often point to symbolic as well as literal meaning, so if we look for other three-day events, we hit upon a comment in Talmud about shiva, the week of mourning after the death of a relative.

Specifically, it says, "Three days for weeping and seven for lamenting" (Moed Katan, 27b). The ancient sages understood the first three days of a loss are the often hardest, with a sadness that can feel unrelenting.

Another interesting detail is what is missing in this plague: There was also no warning to onset of darkness. The other plagues, which brought physical inflictions upon the Mitzrim, were preceded by a warning from Moshe about what would happen.

This begins to paint a picture of a plague which is all too familiar to many of us in the modern world. Look at it again:

The damage wrought by this darkness was symbolic and emotional. It came without warning. It was immobilizing to those experiencing it while those around them were free to move around. It not only blinded the Mitzrim to their surroundings, it also impacted their relationships, as the Torah said, "They did not see each other." In the depth of their affliction, they couldn't even reach out to comfort other sufferers.

In short, the plague of darkness could easily be an analogue for depression.

My point in all of this is to demonstrate that the plagues are more than simplistic morality vignettes. Each one (and indeed, every passage in the Torah) holds meaning that is as relevant to us in our modern age as it was to ancient listeners.

And if the plagues are generally relevant to our lives, how much more so might they relate to our work as monitoring specialists?

The Plagues as Black Swans

Nicolas Taleb first coined the term "Black Swan" to indicate an impossible-to-predict event in finance. I've written elsewhere about the same idea in monitoring, where companies focus time, energy, and money to monitor a single unpredictable event that likely will never recur, instead of addressing simpler issues which, while each incident may have an insignificant impact, are often devastating when looked at in aggregate.

Imagine a discussion of the plagues in a modern IT context, during a meeting with the C-level executives:

"The Nile has turned to blood! We need to set up monitors for water purity and install some environmental indicators for our treatment and filtration plans. That should take care of..." (looks at email) "Wait a minute! Now there seems to be an outbreak of frogs. We need to set up an RFID tracking system to see how far they're spreading. And maybe invest in a natural predator breeding program. Then we can..." (answers phone) "What? Lice! You've got to be kidding me! Okay, let's get the Center for Disease Control on the line..."

You get the point. Each plague is entirely unexpected and unpredictable, and we (with the benefit of having read the Torah—or seen the movie—realize none of the "solutions" will ever address the real problem.

What is the real problem? Like many root causes, it's often a simple issue staring everyone in the face. It's frequently something that has been brought up by in-the-know IT folks at multiple meetings until they are finally shouted down or ignored.

In the case of the Torah, the simple problem is that they need to let the Israelite slaves go. Yes, it might impact the economy. But in the end, not letting them go caused the decimation of the entire country. To be honest, I've seen analogous situations at various companies during my career. (For more information, see my essay on "The Cost of (Not) Monitoring.")

This leads us to another interesting question out of the Torah story: What was Paro thinking? Why didn't he relent after the sixth plague, which brought about painful boils? Or after the seventh plague, the one with the burning hail? A simple translation of the Torah states that "God hardened Paro's heart." This leads many to suggest that God made Paro's heart stone-like when he otherwise would have relented, effectively removing Paro's free will. But, as in so many cases, the original Hebrew indicates a much more nuanced meaning. The text uses the word kavod—which, depending on the vowels, could mean weight, honor, or respect—three times, and in the fourth instance of hardening, the word is chazak (strength). The message in the text is unambiguous: rather than removing free will, God is giving respect to and strengthening Paro's commitment to his chosen course of action, ensuring that he does not waver in the face of mounting pressure.

As a monitoring engineer, you know where I see this in modern times? In the condition called a dollar auction. (I wrote about that here). The dollar auction demonstrates the behavior of people and organizations to be so focused on not losing, that they end up devoting vast and often irrational amounts of time, effort, and money. The more they invest, the less willing they are to walk away from that investment, even when the thing in which they've invested serves them poorly. And nowhere is this so evident as when the incumbent monitoring solution is not serving the needs of the organization, and it's time to cut losses and find a new tool.

Plague after plague, Paro's investment in the Egyptian dollar auction mounted. The more he felt his credibility and reputation was at stake, the less willing he was to consider the cost and consequence of his choices. Customization after customization, patch after patch; the same thing happens in IT organizations across the world.

Where does it end? For the Torah's thought on that, we actually have to go back to the beginning of the Exodus story.

וַיָּקָם מֶלֶךְ-חָדָשׁ, עַל-מִצְרָיִם, אֲשֶׁר לֹא-יָדַע, אֶת-יוֹסֵף

vayakam melech-chadash, al-mitzrayim, asher lo-yada, et yosef
Now there arose a new king over Mitzrayim, who knew not Yosef (Joseph)

Often the only time a company can consider changing their ways is when new leadership enters the picture. A manager who doesn't have a political stake in saying, "This isn't working for us." Whether that happens when the old leaders are booted out–as in the case of Paro after all the plagues–or not, is a choice left entirely up to the leaders themselves.

Question Four: What Alerts Could My Devices Trigger?

It's 3:00 pm. You can see the end of the day peeking at you just over the horizon. You throw a handful of trail mix into your mouth to try to avoid the onset of mid-afternoon-nap-attack syndrome and hope to slide through the next two hours unmolested.

Which, of course, is why you are pulled into a team meeting. Not your team meeting, mind you. It's the Linux server team. On the one hand, you're flattered. They typically don't invite anyone who can't speak fluent Perl or quote every XKCD comic in chronological order (using EPOC time as their reference, of course). On the other hand... #meetings.

As you take a seat, the manager writes the following on the whiteboard:

```
kill `ps -ef | grep -i talking | awk `{print $1}' `
```

This elicits a chorus of laughter from everyone but you. Unfortunately, your conspicuous silence gives the manager the perfect opportunity to focus the conversation uncomfortably on you.

"We have this non-trivial issue and are hoping you can grep out the solution for us," he begins, "because we're responsible for roughly 4,000 systems."

Unable to contain herself, a staff member corrects the manager quickly. She interjects, "4,732 systems. Of which 200 are physical and the remainder are virtualized."

Clearly unimpressed, the manager cuts her off. "Ms. Deal, unless I'm off by an order of magnitude, there's no need to correct."

Chastised, she replies, "Sorry boss."

"As I was saying," he continues. "We have a significant number of systems. Now, how many alerts currently exist in the monitoring system that could generate a ticket?"

Eager to show that you are just as on top of your systems as they are with theirs, you reply with a ready answer. "We have 436 alerts in production, with six currently in active development."

"So how many of those affect our systems?" the manager asks.

Feeling like you are in your element for once, you answer, "Well, not counting tickets you have in the queue right now, pretty much none. If nothing breaches a threshold or throws an error condition, it's safe to say all of your systems are stable. If you want performance data, you can look at each server's detail page for specifics. Of course, with 4,000, I can see how you might want a summary report. We can put something together to show the current statistics, or the average over time, or..."

"You misunderstand," he interrupts. "I'm fully cognizant of the fact that our systems are stable. That's not my question. My question is: if one of my systems becomes unstable, how many of your 436-soon-to-be-442 alerts would trigger for my systems?"

As you process what he's asking, he takes the opportunity to press his point. "As I understand it, alert logic should do two things: first, identify the scope of devices. All Ubuntu systems in the 10.199.1.0/24 subnet, for example. Once the scope is defined, the alert should specify the conditions under which an alert is triggered, say, when the CPU goes over 80 percent for more than 15 minutes."

"So what I want," he concludes, "is a report that shows me only those alerts where the scope includes devices under my team's purview."

Your Mission, Should You Choose to Accept It

As with the other questions we've discussed in this series, the specifics of how to answer this question are actually less critical than being prepared to answer it in the future.

It's also important to understand that this is actually two questions masquerading as one:

1. For each alert, can you show a list the of devices that are potentially in-scope?
2. For each device, can you show a list of the alerts that may potentially be triggered?

This two-part question is perhaps the most important question in this series. Why? Because it determines the scale of the potential notifications that monitoring could generate. It's one thing if five alerts apply to 30 machines. It's entirely another when 30 alerts apply to 4,000 machines. If multiple problems occur at the same time, which they often do, they trigger multiple alerts. This prompts monitoring to generate an unreasonable number of tickets, pages, etc. that have the potential to generate more work than fixing the original problem.

From a business perspective, the answer to this question has implications to staffing, shift allocation, pager rotation, and even the number of alerts a particular team may approve for production.

As with the other questions in this series, the way you go about building this information is going to depend heavily on the monitoring solution you are using.

Some monitoring solutions, often the older, agent-based ones, are sometimes better at this because trigger logic — in the form of an alert name — is pushed down to the agent on each device. This allows you to ask the device, "Hey, what alerts are 'on' you?" You can also ask the alert, "Hey, which devices have you been pushed to?"

However, modern agentless monitoring solutions are able to answer this fairly handily, as well. In fact, more full-featured monitoring tools have options built-in.

Regardless of how you get there, you should check your monitoring solution for reports that look like this:

Summary of Orion Objects: F5; Bas-2621.lab.tex; Net-SNMP; CAI-SQL-01

All Alerts this Object can trigger for Bas-2621.lab.tex
ALL ALERTS

ALERT NAME	DESCRIPTION	SEVERITY	COMMENTS
Alert me when a node reboots	This alert will write to the NetPerfMon event log when the date and time a machine last booted changes	Critical	
High Packet Loss Monitoring(2)	Percent packet loss over the last few minutes. Packet loss is calculated from the number of ICMP packets that are dropped when polling the node. This alert will write to the SolarWinds event log when packet loss rises above 40% and when it drops back below 5%.	Critical	
Alert me when a node goes down	This alert will write to the SolarWinds event log when a node goes down and when a node comes back up again.	Critical	
High Response Time Monitoring(2)	This alert will write to the SolarWinds event log when the average response time for a node goes above 200ms and when the average response time drops back down below 100ms after being above 200ms.	Critical	

All Alerts this Object can trigger for Net-SNMP
ALL ALERTS

ALERT NAME	DESCRIPTION	SEVERITY	COMMENTS
Alert me when a node reboots	This alert will write to the NetPerfMon event log when the date and time a machine last booted changes	Critical	
High Packet Loss Monitoring(2)	Percent packet loss over the last few minutes. Packet loss is calculated from the number of ICMP packets that are dropped when polling the node. This alert will write to the SolarWinds event log when packet loss rises above 40% and when it drops back below 5%.	Critical	
Alert me when a node goes down	This alert will write to the SolarWinds event log when a node goes down and when a node comes back up again.	Critical	
High Response Time Monitoring(2)	This alert will write to the SolarWinds event log when the average response time for a node goes above 200ms and when the average response time drops back down below 100ms after being above 200ms.	Critical	

This shows you each of the alerts that apply to a particular device or group of devices.

The complementary view shows the devices that a specific alert can affect.

Alert Name	Device name	Owner Group
001_Ultimate CPU	dev-aus-lali-02	OrderEntryTeam
	EASTADDS02v	CorpIT
	EASTEXMBX01v	CorpIT
	EASTFILE01v	CorpIT
	NOCDRS01v	NOC
01_BackupCircuitDown	NEWY-2811-WAN	Network-WAN
	EAST-2821-WAN	Network-WAN
	LOSA-2821-WAN	Network-WAN
	WEST-2821-WAN	Network-WAN

It's also nice when your alerting tool incorporates that insight into the alert-building process itself, as in this case:

Houston, We Have a Problem

What if your monitoring tool doesn't have those capabilities built in? What if you have pored through the documentation, opened a ticket with the vendor, visited the online forums, sought counsel from the great guru up on the mountain, and still come back with a big fat goose egg? What then?

Your choices at this point still depend largely on the specific software you are using, but generally speaking there are three options:

Option 1: Reverse-engineer

Many monitoring solutions use a database back-end for the bulk of their metrics, and alerts are simply a query against this data. The alert trigger queries may exist in the database itself, or in a configuration file. Once you have found them, you will need to create a copy of each alert and then go through them, removing the parts comprising the actual trigger (i.e., CPU_Utilization > 80%) and leaving the parts that simply indicate scope (where Vendor = "Microsoft"; where "OperatingSystem" = "Windows 2003"; where "IP_address" contains "10.199.1"; and so on). This will necessitate learning the back-end query language for your tool. Will this be difficult? Probably. Will it increase your street cred with the other users of the tool? Absolutely. Will it save your butt within the first month after you create it? Guaranteed.

The best part is that once you've done the hard work, running a report for each alert becomes extremely simple. You can even set that query to run regularly—weekly or even nightly—and output the information to a separate table from which you can create a report.

Option 2: Create duplicate alerts with no trigger

If you can't export the alert triggers, another option is to create a duplicate of each alert that has the "scope" portion, but not the trigger elements (so the "Windows machines in the 10.199.1.x subnet" part but not the "CPU_Utilization > 80%" part). The only recipient of that alert will be you, and the alert action should be something like writing to a log file with a very simple string ("Alert x has triggered for Device y"). If you are very clever, you can output that information in CSV format so you can import it into a spreadsheet or database for easy consumption. Every so often— every month or quarter—fire off those alerts and then tally up the results that recipient groups can slice and dice.

Option 3: Do it by hand

If all else fails, and the inability to answer this very essential question doesn't cause you to re-evaluate your choice of monitoring tool, you can start documenting by hand. If you know up front that you are in this situation, then it's simply part of the ongoing documentation process. It's going to be a slog, hacking through existing alerts and writing down the trigger information. Hopefully, you can take that trigger info and turn it into an automated query against your existing devices. If not, then I would seriously recommend looking at another tool because in any decent-sized environment, this is not the kind of thing you want to spend your life documenting.

And it's also not something you want to live without.

What Time Is It? Beer o'clock!

After that last meeting — not to mention your whole day — you are ready pack it in. You've successfully navigated the four questions that every monitoring expert is asked:

1. Why did I get that alert?
2. Why didn't I get that alert?
3. What is being monitored on my systems?
4. What alerts might trigger on my systems?

Honestly, if you can do that, there's no reason to fear anything else life throws your way.

The CIO walks up to you on your way to the elevator. "I'm glad I caught up to you," he says, "I just have a quick question."

Just like at Passover, even if we started out knowing there were Four Questions, there are always a few more that pop up during the seder. Continue reading for a bonus fifth question!

How to Handle Being Questioned

Too often in our daily work in IT, being questioned causes us to go on the defense, to look for reasons to reject either the question or the questioner. Challenges to our work, our designs or our processes, even sincere and thoughtful ones, can be hard to respond to dispassionately. It can be emotionally fraught because it inspires fears about one's expertise, reputation, or the result of hours of hard work.

On Pesach (Passover) night, there is a framework that may potentially help us move past those feelings. We find that framework in the narrative of the Four Children. As Rabbi Davidovich mentioned in Chapter Five, they are actually described as four sons in the traditional text, although this has been updated to gender-neutral descriptions in more modern versions of the Haggadah.

חָכָם מָה הוּא אוֹמֵר?
"Chacham mah hu omer?"
"The wise child, what does he ask?"

מַה הָעֵדוֹת וְהַחֻקִּים וְהַמִּשְׁפָּטִים אֲשֶׁר צִוָּה יי אֱלֹהֵינוּ אֶתְכֶם?
"Mah ha-eidot v'hachukim v'hamishpatim, asher tzivah
Adonai Eloheinu etchem?"
"What is the meaning of the laws and traditions God has
commanded?" (Deuteronomy 6:20) is the answer.

And how are we, around the table, expected to answer? The Haggadah supplies us with the words from the Talmud:

וְאַף אַתָּה אֱמָר לוֹ כְּהִלְכוֹת הַפֶּסַח: אֵין מַפְטִירִין אַחַר הַפֶּסַח אֲפִיקוֹמָן.
"V'af atah emor lo k'hilchot hapesach. Ein maftirin achar
hapesach afikoman."
"You should teach him all the traditions of Pesach, even to
the last detail."

The four sons run the gamut of personality types; from smart to stupid, outright rebellious to merely reticent. The Haggadah labels them the wise son, the wicked son, the simple son, and the son who doesn't know how to ask. But because I love alliteration, I'm referring to them here as the Scholar, the Skeptic, the Simple, and the Silent.

Regardless of moniker, each asks their own variation of the same basic question, "What is going on here?" As mentioned before, the Scholar makes a detailed request for detailed answers.

Meanwhile, the Skeptic is standoffish.

מָה הָעֲבֹדָה הַזֹּאת לָכֶם?
"Mah ha-avodah ha-zot lachem?"
"What does this ritual mean to you?"

The Simple child asks simply,

מה זֹּאת?
"Mah zot?"
"What is all this?"

Last of all, there's the Silent child. Perhaps because he's not educated, or perhaps too young, or maybe just shy. Whatever the reason, this last child says nothing at all.

Like the response to the Scholar, the Haggadah records answers to the Skeptic, Simple, and Silent children that each meet them at their place and attempt to move them forward toward understanding.

This leads to the first, and most obvious, lesson the Haggadah provides on this topic: that we need to meet people where they are and proceed from there. Giving the Scholar's answer to the Simple child will not only not answer the question they asked, but it can shut down any possibility of dialogue and further questions.

But this is by no means the only lesson we should take away.

Digging a bit deeper, we see that the rabbis of old had significant discussions about the one child who stood out from the rest, the Skeptic, or wicked son. The other three are presumed to be willing, if not active, participants in the conversation, but the Skeptic gets harsher treatment. "Blunt his teeth," (the plain-text implication being we should punch him in the mouth), and say, "Had you been there, you would not have been saved." On the surface it seems that the response to someone who is skeptical is to push back, put them in their place, and imply that they're not worth the effort.

But that's only on the surface. Quickly, the rabbis of ancient times hit upon another observation: The Skeptic is here. At the table. Asking questions. Sure, he's lacking a few social graces, but if he truly didn't care, why would he show up in the first place? They understand the "blunt his teeth" remark to indicate that we should listen to his words and for the deeper questions they are framing. We should point out that by saying, "What does this mean to you," he is distancing himself from his people, his community, his family. We ask if that's truly what he wants. Because if he really meant to walk away from this discussion, then the whole rich tapestry of tradition goes with it.

Even more telling is the actual answer we give. "It is because of what God did for me when I came out of Egypt." This doesn't sound so radical until you realize that this is the exact same answer we give to the Silent child. Effectively, the authors of the Haggadah may be telling us "blunt his teeth" in our minds and hearts, and hear the question behind the bite. It may also be teaching that under the snarky surface, there may be a simple soul who is just looking for a simple answer to a complex situation.

Dig deeper still and you'll find a lesson that hits at the heart of the problem I identified earlier. This lesson isn't about the imaginary four children at all. It's a pedagogical cautionary tale. To the rabbis, teachers, preachers, tale-spinners, and lesson-givers, the narrative of the four children whispers, "If you are not ready for these and the hundreds of variations of these archetypes, you are not truly ready to teach. Share what you've learned, because Judaism (and, for that matter, IT) values everyone sharing their knowledge, but understand that these are common learning modalities and, as a true teacher, you cannot pick and choose the students who will come to you seeking answers."

This translates to our work as monitoring professionals. If we are not prepared to present, explain, and even defend our solutions to each of the "children," it's incumbent upon us to go back and prepare more diligently, document more clearly, and find additional ways of speaking to both the overarching philosophy of monitoring and the specific details of this implementation. We need to be ready, willing, able, and excited to:

- Answer all the detailed questions of the Scholar and their likely follow-up questions. Be prepared to also provide architecture diagrams, process flows, and unit test results.
- Respond to the Skeptic's challenging questions without rising to the bait that their sharp words might elicit.
- Answer simply when presented with simple questions.
- And finally, explain monitoring in a way that engages the Silent child so they'll be inspired to ask questions of their own.

Question Five: What Do You Monitor Standard?

You think you are going to make it out of the building without another task hanging over your head, but the CIO catches you in the elevator and engages you in a "quick chat" on the way down.

"I'm glad I caught up with you," he says. "I have a quick question."

"I love what you're doing with the monitoring system," he begins, "but one thing that I keep hearing from support teams is that they feel like every new device has to be monitored from the ground up. Is there a way we can just have some monitors in place as soon as it enters the system?"

Choosing your words carefully — it is the CIO, after all — you respond, "Well, there's a whole raft of metrics we collect as soon as any new system is added into monitoring. Then we augment those initial elements with metrics based on what the new device provides, and what the owner and support teams need."

"That's a relief," smiles your CIO, as you arrive at your car. He is now literally standing between you and a well-earned beer. "But our teams, your customers, (Author's Note: This is just one example of why I think the word "customer" is NSFW)," he adds with a chuckle, "need to know what those standard options are. Like when you're buying a new car," he says, eyeing your 2004 rust bucket. "Monitoring should list which features are standard and which are optional upgrades. That shouldn't be too hard, right?"

"Not at all!" you chirp, your enthusiasm having more to do with the fact that he's moved back from your car so you can actually leave, than the work you just inadvertently agreed to do.

"Excellent," he says. "Can you pull it together for me to look over tomorrow?" Without waiting for an answer he walks away, calling, "Have a great night!" over his shoulder.

Grown Organically

"What do you monitor standard?" is a common question because it has a lot to do with how monitoring solutions usually come into being in organizations, how monitoring teams are established, and how conversations between you, the monitoring engineer, and the recipient of monitoring tend to go.

In some cases, monitoring solutions are conceived and implemented as a company-wide initiative with your previous solution in place, but those cases are rare. Instead, it is usually the case that something that started off as a departmental or individual solution was noticed outside the team and extended bit by bit by new groups or individuals. Before long, it becomes the corporate standard. But this approach always creates issues.

"Standard procedure? We do it like this because Harold did it this way when he installed the thing three years ago."

A second point to consider is that monitoring teams are often formed around a specific vendor's solution, such as, "We're experts in product XYZ." They may also form around monitoring for a specific IT silo, such as, "We monitor servers. Networks? Not so much." Unlike more mature IT disciplines like storage, security, or virtualization, people don't usually set out to become monitoring engineers. Therefore, there is little tribal knowledge and precious few courses or books to turn to, in order to help understand how it is usually done. Teams form and, for better or worse, begin to write their own sets of rules.

Finally, largely due to the preceding two points, conversations between the ersatz monitoring engineer and the consumer (the person or team who will read the reports, look at the screens, and receive the alerts) tends to have a number of disconnects. More on that in a moment. But because of these challenging conversations, IT practitioners who could easily take up monitoring as a specialization within the larger IT ecosystem end up being incentivized to remain within their own comfort bubble, whether that is a specific tool or silo, and everyone is poorer for it.

Remaining in their cocoon, the folks who run this homegrown system only work with teams who are already familiar with what they offer, so there's no need to describe monitoring in detail, which creates a barrier to entry for new consumers.

...A Failure to Communicate

Put yourself in the shoes of that new-to-monitoring consumer I mentioned a minute ago.

You've got a new device, application, or service that needs to be monitored. At best, you need it monitored because you realize the value of monitoring. At worst, you need it monitored because you were told your device, application, or service is a Class III critical element to the organization, therefore monitoring is mandatory. You just need to check the little box that says "monitoring" so that you can get this sucker rolled into production.

You make the call and set up a meeting with someone from the vaguely shadowy-sounding Monitoring Team. (What? Do they manage all the keylogger and spyware software you're sure this place is crawling with?) A little while later, you're sitting down in a conference room with them.

You explain your new project, device, application, or service. The person from the Monitoring Team is taking notes, nodding at all the right places. This is looking positive. Then they look up from their notes and ask, "So, what do you need to have monitored here?"

In your head, you're thinking, "I thought you were supposed to tell me that. Why do I have to do all the heavy lifting here?" But you're a professional, so of course you don't say that. Instead, you reply, "Well, I'm sure whatever you monitor standard should be fine."

The monitoring person looks mildly annoyed, and asks "Anything else? I mean, this is a pretty important device/application/service, right?"

So now you do open your mouth. "Well, it's hard to tell since I'm not sure what standard monitoring is!"

"Oh, come on," comes the retort. "You've been using XYZ monitoring for two years now. You know what we monitor on the other stuff for you. It's..."

And then they do the most infuriating thing. They rattle off a list of words. Some of which are components, some are counters, some sound vaguely familiar, and others you've never heard of. And they sit there with their arms crossed, looking at you across the table. *<End Scene>*

This scenario is probably not as dramatic as the ones you've encountered in real life, but it likely captures the essence of the issue. If the monitoring team and those who benefit from monitoring are working from different playbooks, the overall effectiveness of monitoring is going to be impacted.

So, how do you avoid this? Or, if you've already fallen into friction, how do you get past it? As with the rest of this series, I have a few answers that begin with, "Knowing that you will be asked this question is half the battle." Once you accept that, you can prepare for the rest.

But the daemon, as they say, is in the details. So, let's dig in!

好记性不如烂笔头

Translation: A good memory is no match for a bad pen nub.

My first suggestion? Make sure you have solid documentation.

Before you start quaking at the thought of mountains of research, keep in mind that that you aren't documenting the specific thresholds, values, etc. for each node. You are compiling a list of the default instrumentation that is enabled when a new system is added to your monitoring solution. Depending on your software, that could be a consistent list—regardless of device type—or it could be a core set of common values and a few additional variations by device type.

The first thing you should always do is Read The Friendly Manual (RTFM). Many vendors have already done this work for you, so all you need to do is copy and paste that into your documentation.

If your vendor considers such information to be legally protected intellectual property, your next step is to simply look at the screens themselves. I mean, it's not that hard. After scanning a couple of the detail pages for devices, you're going to see a pattern emerge. It will probably be something like:

- Availability
  - Response time
  - Packet loss
- CPU
  - Overall percent utilization, five-minute average
  - Per processor percent utilization, five-minute average
- Physical RAM
  - Percent utilization, five-minute average
  - IO Operations Per Second (IOPS)
  - Errors
- Virtual RAM
  - Percent utilization, five-minute average
  - IO Operations Per Second (IOPS)
  - Errors

- Disk
  - Availability
  - Capacity
  - Used
  - IOPS
- Interface
  - Availability
  - Bandwidth
    - Bits per second (BPS)
    - Percent Utilization
    - Packets Per Second (PPS)
  - Errors
  - Discards

There, in that relatively short list, you will likely find the core of the metrics that every machine provides. Then you have specifics for routers, including flapping routes, VPN metrics, etc.; switches, including stacked switch cabling status, VLAN availability and performance, etc.; virtual machines, including host statistics, noisy neighbor events; and so on.

When all else fails, there's always Wireshark®. By monitoring the connection between the monitoring system and a single target device – preferably one you have recently added – you can capture all communication and figure out the metrics being requested and supplied. It's not pretty, it might not even be easy, but it's a lot easier than having to repeatedly tell your colleagues that you have no idea what gets monitored.

P.S. If you are out of other options and down to Wireshark as your final choice, it's a good sign that it's time to look at another monitoring solution.

There's an App for That

Everything I've so far is great for hardware-based metrics, including specialized storage and virtualization tools. But once you cross into the valley of the shadow of application monitoring, you need a better strategy.

By its very nature, application monitoring is highly customized, with a huge level of variability from one application to another. Take something as straightforward as Microsoft® Exchange™. When building a monitoring solution, you might need specific monitoring for the hub transport server, the mailbox server, the client access server, or even the external OWA server (just to name a few). Do you monitor the POP3 service, or just IMAPI? It all depends on your implementation. While there are common elements from one to the other, they serve very different purposes and require very different components and thresholds.

Take that level of variability and multiply it by all the applications in your environment and you can start to appreciate the level of work you are looking at.

So, what is the diligent, yet slightly overwhelmed monitoring engineer to do? Movies like Glengarry Glen Ross and The Boiler Room have popularized the phrase, ABC, or Always Be Closing, within sales circles. In monitoring, and indeed, within much of IT, I prefer ABS, or Always Be Standardizing.

Whether it's alerts, reports, or sets of application monitoring components, the best thing you can do for yourself is continuously attempt to create a single gold standard for a particular need, and continue using it. Expand that single standard when necessary to account for additional variations, but avoid, as much as possible, the copy-and-paste process that leaves you with 42 different Exchange monitoring templates. You'll be glad you did when, 18 months down the road, you can easily pinpoint the default, and quickly recognize which ones are applied to which server.

If you are able to adhere to this one practice, then answering the question, "What do you monitor standard?" becomes immeasurably more achievable.

Good Monitoring is its Own Reward

Let's take a look at how different the conversation I described at the beginning of this chapter looks now that you have more information. Once again, put yourself in their shoes:

You explain your situation by saying, "We need you to monitor about 20 of our devices and the applications that go with them."

"Great!" they say. "It's a good thing you're talking to me and not accounts receivable! Do you have a list of what you are putting together?"

You laugh politely at their very not funny joke and say, "Right here."

They review the document, and then say, "Okay, great. I've got a list here of the things that get monitored automatically when we load your devices into our solution. Can you take a look and tell me if anything is missing that you think is important to include?" They provide a list of default systems monitors.

You scan the list and, honestly, you are impressed. "Wow. This is... a lot. It's more than we expected. We don't want tickets on all this."

They quickly clarify, "Oh, no. These are the metrics we collect. Alerts are something else. But if you need to see the general health of your systems, this is what we can provide you automatically."

"Oh, I get it!" you say. "That's great. You know what? We'll ride with this list for the time being."

"Perfect. Now, on the application side, we've actually worked with a few projects that use roughly the same platform as yours. Here's what we have in place today." They provide a separate list of application monitoring.

You take a look and, while it's comprehensive, it's not complete. "Okay. I can already see we'll need a few extra items that the developers have said they want to track. They will also want to alert on some custom messages they're generating."

"No worries," they say, "You can get me that list by email later, if you want. I'm sure we'll be able to get it all set up for you."

Very appreciative now, you are honestly enthusiastic about getting this done. "Wow, this was a lot less painful than we expected."

They humbly respond, "I know!"

Had Gadya - The Law of Unintended Consequences

"Then came the angel of death; who killed the butcher, who had slaughtered the ox, who had drank the water, who had quenched the fire..."

At the end of the night, after all the wine has been drunk and the last bit of matzah has been eaten; after ending the seder with the declaration of hope that we all meet l'shana haba'ah b'yerushalayim ("next year in Jerusalem," or "in an age of universal peace and unity"); even as some of your guests dig in the closet for their coats to begin the long trek home, while others begin to clear dishes and look longingly toward their beds; there are still those who linger at the table and continue to share Passover ideas, whose themes carry far beyond this one holiday.

Rather than telling stories or relating bits of scriptural text, the information at this point in the seder takes the form of songs. Seemingly innocent, they carry lessons that are based in history, but which are deeply relevant to our present-day situations. One such song is Had Gadya, or One Little Goat. Had Gadya chronicles the way one odd thing happens after another, a theme repeated in other songs from other cultures.

It starts simply enough:

One little goat, one little goat:
My father bought for two zuzim,
one little goat, one little goat.

But then things immediately go wrong:

Then came the cat
that ate the goat
My father bought for two zuzim
One little goat, one little goat

Before long, events take an odd twist, shifting from the natural order to include inanimate objects:

Then came the stick
that beat the dog
that bit the cat...
Near the end, things have taken the darkest of turns:
Then came the Angel of Death
Who killed the butcher
That slaughtered the ox
That drank the water...
And then, out of nowhere, literally a Deus Ex Machina:
Then came the Holy One, Blessed Be He
Who slew the Angel of Death
who killed the butcher
who slaughtered the ox
that drank the water
that quenched the fire
that burnt the stick
that beat the dog
that bit the cat
that ate the goat
my father bought for two zuzim
one little goat, one little goat

The simple pattern of the song, with verses that build upon each other as the song begins each cycle, delights both the young and the young at heart. But—as with everything else in the Passover seder—there are hidden lessons if you only take a moment to look a little deeper.

The instigator of this song is something small. Just a little goat purchased for a few coins. Immediately, there are unanticipated reactions to this seemingly trivial start: A predator comes and eats the goat, then a higher-order predator comes onto the scene. Then things take a metaphorical turn. It seems like there's always another shoe to drop, or in this case, a stick to fall on the unsuspecting hindquarters of the dog. Only after events progress do we see how inextricably entwined everything is. And once the dominoes begin falling in earnest, when there's no stopping them, only then is it clear that nothing short of a miracle can stop things from continuing to ever more tragic ends.

How many times in IT have we watched as small errors are ignored, and that things have to get worse before they can get better.

"It was only one firewall..."
"It was just a small application subroutine..."
"It was a tiny cabling error..."

In computing, it has never been truer: Everything in your environment, no matter how small, has the potential to affect—and be affected by—anything and everything else.

Most people in your organization are like all of us at the beginning of the song—happy with the cute little goat (or IoT device, or cloud service) our father purchased. We cannot possibly predict the cascade of failures that will ultimately bring us face to face with our Maker. It is only we who practice the discipline of monitoring; we who can recite the litany of failures we've seen over the years; it is only those of us in the know who intuitively understand how very wrong seemingly simple things can go.

Passover offers the following important lesson: Those of us who have gained valuable insight from difficult experiences have an obligation to infuse the cultural DNA of the companies for whom we work with the understanding of downstream consequences. And one simple way to do that is to sing the song of our experience often and with great humor, until even the simplest among our team can recite it by heart.

Summary

You pull into the driveway and walk to your door, reflecting on how 8:45 am seemed like 100 years ago. In just one day you've put countless miles on that old brain of yours. You go inside, sit down, and take a minute to clear your head. That's when you have an IT epiphany.

First, you realize that monitoring, good monitoring, is something that is achievable by anyone willing to put in a little time and effort. You see that can achieve monitoring success using the monitoring solutions which are readily available, quickly installable, and easily maintainable. This is especially true because solid, full-featured, enterprise-class monitoring solutions are more affordable now than they've ever been.

Second, you understand that putting in the time and effort to create good monitoring makes your job significantly more enjoyable.

Third, you recognize that monitoring should be treated as a separate discipline within IT. It is as valid a sub-specialty as networking, programming, storage, virtualization, or information security. Furthermore, when it is treated as a discipline, people are more willing to put in the time and effort to invest in the tools that help make monitoring possible.

Fourth, and finally, you appreciate that everything that happened today–from the first question you answered early this morning, all the way to the cold beer you have in your hand now–is all part of a day's work in IT.

> Over the course of the Passover Seder, we drink four glasses of wine. In Judaism, wine does not serve any sacramental function. It doesn't imbue a prayer or rite with any extra holiness, nor does it create a connection to the divine. Simply put, wine represents joy. It is there to symbolize the joy we hope to feel at the Passover seder, and to facilitate it.

The message to folks working in technology-related fields is that it is important—essential, in fact—to recognize and celebrate moments of success, whether they are great achievements or small victories. Too often, we fall into the trap of completing a task or fixing an issue and moving on to the next without pause, without reflection, without taking even a moment to bask in the feeling of satisfaction you get when you have accomplished something. We forget to allow ourselves some small measure of joy.

But these four cups of fermented joy carry with them a significant measure of symbolism. Ancient debates focus on whether we should drink four cups or five; which part of the meal each cup belongs to; the blessings that can or cannot be said over each cup; and more.

IT practitioners will be quick to note that the fact that these things have been hotly debated for millennia speak to the importance of standards, and the clear communication of those standards.

These debates are more than just academic exercises in intellectual curiosity. Judaism teaches that we are obligated—commanded—to observe the Passover seder and all its component parts. Because it is a command and not simply a nice idea, our specificity matters, or should matter to us if we are taking it seriously.

Too many of us have been in meetings with business leaders who fail to understand the real, measurable, actual value that monitoring brings to their company. It's not for lack of proof that monitoring is worthwhile. It's because, for whatever set of reasons, the leaders haven't chosen to value its importance. This makes our work as monitoring professionals infinitely more difficult.

And this gets at an even deeper lesson, one that pervades Jewish thought to its very core: the pursuit of אֱמֶת - emet, or "Truth" with a capital T. For a religion, Judaism is remarkably un-interested in feelings. What I mean is that what you believe in your gut about a particular observance, or story from the Torah, is irrelevant to the objective truth of it. You are free, of course, to believe or disbelieve; if you are not convinced, you are encouraged to discuss, debate, and research the point. But not liking, not appreciating, or not believing in a commandment does not excuse someone from observing it.

That's not to say that every point of Jewish law is completely understood. There are rulings that remain effectively unresolved—a couple dozen or so out of thousands—which brings us back to the four or five cups of wine.

The debate is more than just personal opinion. In matters of Jewish law, there are well-defined rules for figuring out which of multiple differing views is correct. For example, a decision made by an earlier generation of scholars cannot be overturned by a later generation, but it can be adapted to account for current conditions or realities. Meanwhile, within a single generation, certain scholars are acknowledged to be consistently correct while others less so.

Several of these rules clash when it comes to the four or five cups, which creates the uncertainty. In our modern existence, when so much of the context and background knowledge of the original conversations has faded from memory, we simply don't know. Our job is to keep asking, keep discussing, keep studying in the hope that we'll eventually find closure, while at the same time accepting that we—as individuals as well as humans on this earth—will never know the answer to all things.

We can take many lessons from this. For one, saying, "I don't know" is not the end, but the beginning. Even saying, "I cannot know; the source code is lost," is still not the end. And if you inherited an old design, it is best to honor the folks who did the hard work of creating it, not dismissing them or the design because it is old.

It's true that technology is not the same as religion. In IT we can, and sometimes should, get rid of outmoded ways of working and thinking. But I believe that sometimes we do so too quickly, and lose touch with some of the core values, stories, and lessons that are wrapped up in that old tech.

As we sit back and sip that last glass of wine, it's a lesson worth considering.

Appendix I: Hebrew Names and Their Meanings

Below you will find a quick reference to the names and words that appear in this book, but have origins in the Torah, midrash (stories that enhance or explain the Torah narrative), halacha (Jewish law), and more.

Hebrew Name/Term	English Name or Extended Description	Literal Hebrew Meaning
Aharon	Aaron	Exalted
B'nei Yisrael	Israelites	Children of Yisrael
Choshech	Plague of Darkness	Darkness
Chametz	Leavened or leavened products. This food group is forbidden on Pesach.	Leavened, also "pride"
Eichah	Book of Lamentations	How, or "How could it be?" (The opening verse of the Book of Lamentations)
Had Gadya	One Little Goat	Song traditionally sung toward the end of the Seder
Hagaddah	The book that explains the order of the Pesach Seder	Telling
Matzah	Unleavened bread eaten at the Seder and throughout Pesach	
Maggid	The main part of the Seder. This is point at which most of the stories are told and questions are asked.	The Teller
Mitzrayim/Mitzrim	Egypt/Egyptians	The narrow place
Moshe	Moses	Drawn from the water, also the Egyptian word for "child"
Paroh	Pharaoh	King of Egypt
Pesach	Passover	Jumped over, or skipped

Pirkei Avos	Ethics of Our Fathers	A tractate in the Talmud that deals primarily with ethical issues
Seder	Passover Meal	Order
Shabbos	Sabbath	Rest
Shul	Synagogue	School (Yiddish)
Tisha B'Av	9th of Av	Day of mourning for the destruction of the Holy Temple
Yaakov	Jacob	Heel-grabber
Yam Suf	Red Sea	Red Sea, or "Reed Sea"
Yisrael	Israel	Struggled with God, also Yaakov's other name
Yirmiyahu	Jeremiah	Raised by God
Yosef	Joseph	He will increase

About the Authors

Leon Adato

In a career spanning three decades and four countries, Leon Adato has been an actor, electrician, carpenter, stage combat instructor, pest control technician, Sunday school teacher, and ASL interpreter. He also occasionally worked on computers.

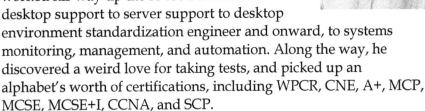

Leon got his start teaching computer classes, worked his way up the IT food chain from desktop support to server support to desktop environment standardization engineer and onward, to systems monitoring, management, and automation. Along the way, he discovered a weird love for taking tests, and picked up an alphabet's worth of certifications, including WPCR, CNE, A+, MCP, MCSE, MCSE+I, CCNA, and SCP.

Leon spent almost 20 years honing his monitoring skills at companies that ranged in scale from modest (10-100 systems), to moderate (1-3,000 systems) to ludicrous (250,000 systems in 5,000 locations), becoming proficient with a variety of tools and solutions along the way

If you are interested in seeing, hearing, or reading more of his work, here are some ways to find out more:

- Website: https://www.adatosystems.com
- Podcast: https://www.technicallyreligious.com/
- Twitter: https://www.twitter.com/leonadato

Rabbi Raphael Davidovich

Rabbi Davidovich is a native of Montreal. He is a musmach of Ner Israel Rabbinical College in Baltimore, where he also served as a rabbinic intern at Congregation Shomrei Emunah under Rabbi Dr. Tzvi Hirsh Weinreb. He was rabbi of Adath Jeshurun Congregation in Newport News, Virginia, from 2001 until he came to HJC in September of 2006. The Rabbi and his wife Deena have five children.

Visit his website: http://thisshiurisaboutyou.wordpress.com